CONTENTS

D1064030

WHY A LOW FAT DIET?

We need a certain amount of fat in our diet for general health and it is a valuable source of energy. Also, it plays a vital role in making foods palatable to eat. However, most of us eat more fat than we need. You should not try to cut out fat altogether, but a lower fat diet has the benefits of weight loss and reduction in the risk of heart disease.

There are two types of fat – saturated and unsaturated. The unsaturated group includes two types – polyunsaturated and monounsaturated fats.

Saturated fats are the ones you should limit, as they increase cholesterol in the blood, and this can increase the risk of heart disease. The main sources of saturated fat are animal products such as dairy products and meat, but also hard fats and hydrogenated vegetable fat or oil. Polyunsaturated fats are essential in small quantities for good health, and are thought to help reduce the cholesterol in the blood. There is also some evidence that monounsaturated fats have a beneficial effect. The main sources of polyunsaturates are vegetable oils such as sunflower, corn and soya, and oily fish such as herring, mackerel, pilchards, sardines and trout. Sources of monounsaturated fats include olive, rapeseed and groundnut oils, as well as avocadoes and many nuts.

Cutting Down on Cholesterol?

Cholesterol is a substance which occurs naturally in the blood, and is essential for the formation of hormones, body cells, nerves and bile salts which help digestion.

A high cholesterol level can increase the likelihood of coronary heart disease, as it becomes deposited on the walls of the arteries, causing them to fur up. The main cause of raised cholesterol levels is eating too much fat, especially saturated fat. Eating too much saturated fat encourages the body to make more cholesterol than it needs, and also seems to prevent it getting rid of the excess.

The cholesterol found in foods such as egg yolk, offal, cheese, butter and shellfish does not have a major effect on the amount of blood cholesterol in most people, but it is best not to eat large quantities of these foods too often.

Fresh approach: when you are shopping for low fat foods, choose fresh seasonal vegetables (top right) and cook them without added fat. Salads (right) are a good accompaniment too, just use a polyunsaturated or monounsaturated oil for the dressing. Fresh fruits (above) are the perfect ending to a low fat meal if you haven't time to cook – eat them either raw in a salad or poach in fruit juice and serve hot with yogurt.

EASY WAYS TO CUT DOWN FAT AND SATURATED FAT

EAT LESS	TRY INSTEAD
Butter and hard fats.	Try spreading butter more thinly, or replace it with a low fat spread or polyunsaturated margarine.
Fatty meats and high fat products such as pies and sausages.	Buy the leanest cuts of meat you can afford and choose low fat meats like skinless chicken or turkey. Look for reduced-fat sausages and meat products. Eat fish more often, especially oily fish.
Full fat dairy products like cream, butter, hard margarine, milk and hard cheeses.	Choose skimmed or semi-skimmed milk and milk products, and try low fat yogurt, low fat fromage frais and lower fat cheeses such as skimmed milk soft cheese, reduced fat Cheddar, mozzarella or Brie.
Hard cooking fats such as lard or hard margarine.	Choose polyunsaturated oils for cooking, such as olive, sunflower, corn or soya oil.
Rich salad dressings like mayonnaise or salad cream.	Make salad dressings with low fat yogurt or fromage frais, or use a healthy oil such as olive oil.
Fried foods.	Grill, microwave, steam or bake when possible. Roast meats on a rack. Fill up on starchy foods like pasta, rice and couscous. Choose jacket or boiled potatoes, not chips.
Added fat in cooking.	Use heavy-based or non-stick pans so you can cook with little or no added fat.
High fat snacks such as crisps, chocolate, cakes, pastries and biscuits.	Choose fresh or dried fruit, breadsticks or vegetable sticks. Make your own low fat cakes and bakes.

INDEX

STARTERS
AND SNACKS

APRICOT YOGURT COOKIES

These soft cookies are very quick to make and are useful for the biscuit tin or for lunch boxes.

INGREDIENTS

Makes 16

175g/6oz/1½ cups plain flour
5ml/1 tsp baking powder
5ml/1 tsp ground cinnamon
75g/3oz/1 cup rolled oats
75g/3oz/½ cup light muscovado sugar
115g/4oz/½ cup chopped ready-to-eat
    dried apricots
15ml/1 tbsp flaked hazelnuts or
    almonds
150g/5oz/⅔ cup natural yogurt
45ml/3 tbsp sunflower oil
demerara sugar, to sprinkle

1 Preheat the oven to 190°C/375°F/ Gas 5. Lightly oil a large baking sheet.

2 Sift together the flour, baking powder and cinnamon. Stir in the oats, sugar, apricots and nuts.

3 Beat together the yogurt and oil, then stir evenly into the mixture to make a firm dough. If necessary, add a little more yogurt.

4 Use your hands to roll the mixture into about 16 small balls, place on the baking sheet and flatten with a fork.

5 Sprinkle with demerara sugar. Bake for 15–20 minutes, or until firm and golden brown. Leave to cool on a wire rack.

COOK'S TIP
These cookies do not keep well, so it is best to eat them within two days, or to freeze them. Pack into polythene bags and freeze for up to four months.

NUTRITION NOTES

Per portion:

Energy	95Kcals/400kJ
Fat	2.66g
Saturated fat	0.37g
Cholesterol	0.3mg
Fibre	0.94g

MELON AND BASIL SOUP

A deliciously refreshing, chilled fruit soup, just right for a hot summer's day. It takes next to no time to prepare, leaving you free to enjoy the sunshine and, even better, it is almost totally fat-free.

INGREDIENTS

Serves 4–6
2 Charentais or rock melons
75g/3oz/6 tbsp caster sugar
175ml/6fl oz/¾ cup water
finely grated rind and juice of 1 lime
45ml/3 tbsp shredded fresh basil
fresh basil leaves, to garnish

1 Cut the melons in half across the middle. Scrape out the seeds and discard. Using a melon baller, scoop out 20–24 balls and set aside for the garnish. Scoop out the remaining flesh and place in a blender or food processor. Set aside.

2 Place the sugar, water and lime zest in a small pan over a low heat. Stir until dissolved, bring to the boil and simmer for 2–3 minutes. Remove from the heat and leave to cool slightly. Pour half the mixture into the blender or food processor with the melon flesh. Blend until smooth, adding the remaining syrup and lime juice to taste.

3 Pour the mixture into a bowl, stir in the basil and chill. Serve garnished with basil leaves and melon balls.

NUTRITION NOTES	
Per portion:	
Energy	69Kcals/293.8kJ
Fat	0.14g
Saturated Fat	0
Cholesterol	0
Fibre	0.47g

COOK'S TIP
Add the syrup in two stages, as the amount of sugar needed will depend on the sweetness of the melon.

OATY CRISPS

These biscuits are very crisp and
crunchy – ideal to serve with
morning coffee.

INGREDIENTS

Makes 18

175g/6oz/1¾ cups rolled oats
75g/3oz/½ cup light muscovado
　sugar
1 egg
60ml/4 tbsp sunflower oil
30ml/2 tbsp malt extract

NUTRITION NOTES

Per portion:
Energy	86Kcals/360kJ
Fat	3.59g
Saturated Fat	0.57g
Cholesterol	10.7mg
Fibre	0.66g

1 Preheat the oven to 190°C/375°F/
Gas 5. Lightly grease two baking
sheets. Mix the rolled oats and sugar in
a bowl, breaking up any lumps in the
sugar. Add the egg, sunflower oil and
malt extract, mix well, then leave to
soak for 15 minutes.

2 Using a teaspoon, place small heaps
of the mixture well apart on the
prepared baking sheets. Press the heaps
into 7.5cm/3in rounds with the back of
a dampened fork.

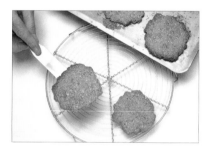

3 Bake the biscuits for 10–15 minutes
until golden brown. Leave them to
cool for 1 minute, then remove with a
palette knife and cool on a wire rack.

COOK'S TIP
To give these biscuits a coarser
texture, substitute jumbo oats for
some or all of the rolled oats.
Once cool, store the biscuits in an
airtight container to keep them as
crisp and fresh as possible.

ITALIAN VEGETABLE SOUP

The success of this clear soup depends on the quality of the stock, so for the best results, be sure you use home-made vegetable stock rather than stock cubes.

INGREDIENTS

Serves 4

1 small carrot
1 baby leek
1 celery stick
50g/2oz green cabbage
900ml/1½ pints/3¾ cups vegetable stock
1 bay leaf
115g/4oz/1 cup cooked cannellini or
*   haricot beans*
25g/1oz/⅕ cup soup pasta, such as tiny
*   shells, bows, stars or elbows*
salt and black pepper
snipped fresh chives, to garnish

1 Cut the carrot, leek and celery into 5cm/2in long julienne strips. Slice the cabbage very finely.

NUTRITION NOTES

Per portion:

Energy	69Kcals/288kJ
Protein	3.67g
Fat	0.71g
Saturated Fat	0.05g
Fibre	2.82g

2 Put the stock and bay leaf into a large saucepan and bring to the boil. Add the carrot, leek and celery, cover and simmer for 6 minutes.

3 Add the cabbage, beans and pasta shapes. Stir, then simmer uncovered for a further 4–5 minutes, or until the vegetables and pasta are tender.

4 Remove the bay leaf and season with salt and pepper to taste. Ladle into four soup bowls and garnish with snipped chives. Serve immediately.

RASPBERRY MUFFINS

These American muffins are made using baking powder and low fat buttermilk, giving them a light and spongy texture. They are delicious to eat at any time of the day.

INGREDIENTS

Makes 10–12
275g/10oz/2½ cups plain flour
15ml/1 tbsp baking powder
115g/4oz/½ cup caster sugar
1 egg
250ml/8fl oz/1 cup buttermilk
60ml/4 tbsp sunflower oil
150g/5oz raspberries

NUTRITION NOTES

Per muffin:
Energy	171Kcals/719kJ
Fat	4.55g
Saturated Fat	0.71g
Cholesterol	16.5mg
Fibre	1.02g

1 Preheat the oven to 200°C/400°F/ Gas 6. Arrange 12 paper cake cases in a deep muffin tin. Sift the flour and baking powder into a mixing bowl, stir in the sugar, then make a well in the centre.

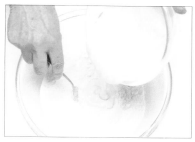

2 Mix the egg, buttermilk and sun-flower oil together in a bowl, pour into the flour mixture and mix quickly.

3 Add the raspberries and lightly fold in with a metal spoon. Spoon the mixture into the paper cases.

4 Bake the muffins for 20–25 minutes until golden brown and firm in the middle. Transfer to a wire rack and serve warm or cold.

CHICKEN AND PASTA SOUP

INGREDIENTS

Serves 4–6
900ml/1½ pints/3¾ cups chicken stock
1 bay leaf
4 spring onions, sliced
225g/8oz button mushrooms, sliced
115g/4oz cooked chicken breast
50g/2oz soup pasta
150ml/¼ pint/⅔ cup dry white wine
15ml/1 tbsp chopped fresh parsley
salt and black pepper

NUTRITION NOTES

Per portion:
Energy	126Kcals/529kJ
Fat	2.2g
Saturated Fat	0.6g
Cholesterol	19mg
Fibre	1.3g

1 Put the stock and bay leaf into a pan and bring to the boil.

2 Add the spring onions and mushrooms to the stock.

3 Remove the skin from the chicken and slice the meat thinly using a sharp knife. Add to the soup and season to taste. Heat through for about 2–3 minutes.

4 Add the pasta, cover and simmer for 7–8 minutes. Just before serving, add the wine and chopped parsley, heat through for 2–3 minutes, then season to taste.

DATE AND APPLE MUFFINS

You will only need one or two of these wholesome muffins per person, as they are very filling.

INGREDIENTS

Makes 12
150g/5oz/1¼ cups self-raising
  wholemeal flour
150g/5oz/1¼ cups self-raising
  white flour
5ml/1 tsp ground cinnamon
5ml/1 tsp baking powder
25g/1 oz/2 tbsp soft margarine
75g/3oz/½ cup light muscovado sugar
1 eating apple
250ml/8fl oz/1 cup apple juice
30ml/2 tbsp pear and apple spread
1 egg, lightly beaten
75g/3oz/½ cup chopped dates
15ml/1 tbsp chopped pecan nuts

1 Preheat the oven to 200°C/400°F/ Gas 6. Arrange 12 paper cake cases in a deep muffin tin. Put the wholemeal flour in a mixing bowl. Sift in the white flour with the cinnamon and baking powder. Rub in the margarine until the mixture resembles breadcrumbs, then stir in the muscovado sugar.

2 Quarter and core the apple, chop the flesh finely and set aside. Stir a little of the apple juice with the pear and apple spread until smooth. Mix in the remaining juice, then add to the rubbed-in mixture with the egg. Add the chopped apple to the bowl with the dates. Mix quickly until just combined.

3 Divide the mixture among the muffin cases.

4 Sprinkle with the chopped pecan nuts. Bake the muffins for 20–25 minutes until golden brown and firm in the middle. Remove to a wire rack and serve while still warm.

NUTRITION NOTES

Per muffin:
Energy	163Kcals/686kJ
Fat	2.98g
Saturated Fat	0.47g
Cholesterol	16.04mg
Fibre	1.97g

COOK'S TIP
Use a pear in place of the eating apple and chopped ready-to-eat dried apricots in place of the dates. Ground mixed spice is a good alternative to cinnamon.

SPICY TOMATO AND LENTIL SOUP

Serves 4

15ml/1 tbsp sunflower oil
1 onion, finely chopped
1–2 garlic cloves, crushed
2.5cm/1in piece fresh root ginger,
*   peeled and finely chopped*
5ml/1 tsp cumin seeds, crushed
450g/1lb ripe tomatoes, peeled, seeded
*   and chopped*
115g/4oz/½ cup red split lentils
1.2 litres/2 pints/5 cups vegetable or
*   chicken stock*
15ml/1 tbsp tomato purée
salt and black pepper
low fat natural yogurt and chopped
*   fresh parsley, to garnish (optional)*

1 Heat the sunflower oil in a large heavy-based saucepan and cook the chopped onion gently for 5 minutes until softened.

2 Stir in the garlic, ginger and cumin, followed by the tomatoes and lentils. Cook over a low heat for a further 3–4 minutes.

3 Stir in the stock and tomato purée. Bring to the boil, then lower the heat and simmer gently for about 30 minutes until the lentils are soft. Season to taste with salt and pepper.

4 Purée the soup in a blender or food processor. Return to the clean pan and reheat gently. Serve in heated bowls. If liked, garnish each portion with a swirl of yogurt and a little chopped parsley.

NUTRITION NOTES	
Per portion:	
Energy	165Kcals/695kJ
Fat	4g
Saturated Fat	0.5g
Cholesterol	0

PINEAPPLE AND CINNAMON DROP SCONES

Making the batter with pineapple juice instead of milk cuts down on fat and adds to the taste.

INGREDIENTS

Makes 24

115g/4oz/1 cup self-raising wholemeal flour
115g/4oz/1 cup self-raising white flour
5ml/1 tsp ground cinnamon
15ml/1 tbsp caster sugar
1 egg
300ml/½ pint/1¼ cups pineapple juice
75g/3oz/½ cup semi-dried pineapple, chopped

NUTRITION NOTES

Per portion:	
Energy	15Kcals/215kJ
Fat	0.81g
Saturated Fat	0.14g
Cholesterol	8.02mg
Fibre	0.76g

1 Preheat a griddle, heavy-based frying pan or an electric frying pan. Put the wholemeal flour in a mixing bowl. Sift in the white flour, add the cinnamon and sugar and make a well in the centre.

> COOK'S TIP
> Drop scones do not keep well and are best eaten freshly cooked. Other semi-dried fruit, such as apricots or pears, can be used in place of the pineapple.

2 Add the egg with half the pineapple juice and gradually incorporate the surrounding flour to make a smooth batter. Beat in the remaining juice with the chopped pineapple.

3 Lightly grease the griddle or pan. Drop tablespoons of the batter on to the surface, leaving them until they bubble and the bubbles begin to burst.

4 Turn the drop scones with a palette knife and cook until the underside is golden brown. Keep the cooked scones warm and moist by wrapping them in a clean napkin while continuing to cook successive batches.

SPINACH AND BEAN CURD SOUP

This appetizing clear soup has an extremely delicate and mild flavour that can be used as a perfect counterbalance to the intense heat of a hot Thai curry.

INGREDIENTS

Serves 6

30ml/2 tbsp dried shrimps
1 litre/1¾ pints/4 cups chicken stock
225g/8oz fresh bean curd, drained and
    cut into 2cm/¾in cubes
30ml/2 tbsp fish sauce
350g/12oz fresh spinach, washed
    thoroughly
black pepper
2 spring onions, finely sliced, to garnish

1 Rinse and drain the dried shrimps. Combine the shrimps with the chicken stock in a large saucepan and bring to the boil.

2 Add the bean curd and simmer for about 5 minutes. Season with fish sauce and black pepper to taste.

3 Tear the spinach leaves into bite-size pieces and add to the soup. Cook for another 1–2 minutes.

4 Remove from the heat and sprinkle with the finely sliced spring onions, to garnish.

NUTRITION NOTES	
Per portion:	
Energy	64Kcals/270kJ
Fat	225g
Saturated Fat	0.26g
Cholesterol	25mg
Fibre	1.28g

COOK'S TIP
Home-made chicken stock makes the world of difference to clear soups. Accumulate enough bones to make a big batch of stock, use what you need and keep the rest in the freezer.

Put 1.5kg/3–3½lb meaty chicken bones and 450g/1lb pork bones (optional) into a large saucepan. Add 3 litres/5 pints/12 cups water and slowly bring to the boil. Occasionally skim off and discard any scum that rises to the surface. Add 2 slices fresh root ginger, 2 garlic cloves (optional), 2 celery sticks, 4 spring onions, 2 bruised lemon grass stalks, a few sprigs of coriander and 10 crushed black peppercorns. Reduce the heat to low and simmer for about 2–2½ hours.

Remove from the heat and leave to cool, uncovered and undisturbed. Pour through a fine strainer, leaving the last dregs behind as they tend to cloud the soup. Leave to cool, then chill. Use as required, removing any fat that congeals on the surface.

CHOCOLATE AND BANANA BROWNIES

Nuts traditionally give brownies their chewy texture. Here oat bran is used instead, creating a low fat, moist, moreish, yet healthy alternative.

INGREDIENTS

Serves 9

75ml/5 tbsp reduced fat cocoa powder
15ml/1 tbsp caster sugar
75ml/5 tbsp skimmed milk
3 large bananas, mashed
215g/7½oz/1 cup soft light brown sugar
5ml/1 tsp vanilla essence
5 egg whites
75g/3oz/¾ cup self-raising flour
75g/3oz/¾ cup oat bran
15ml/1 tbsp icing sugar, for dusting

NUTRITION NOTES

Per portion:

Energy	230Kcals/968kJ
Fat	2.15g
Saturated Fat	0.91g
Fibre	1.89g

COOK'S TIPS
Store these brownies in an airtight tin for a day before eating – they improve with keeping.

You'll find reduced fat cocoa powder in health food stores. If you can't find it, ordinary cocoa powder will work just as well, but, of course, the fat content will be much higher!

1 Preheat the oven to 180°C/350°F/ Gas 4. Line a 20cm/8in square tin with non-stick baking paper.

2 Blend the reduced fat cocoa powder and caster sugar with the skimmed milk. Add the bananas, soft light brown sugar and vanilla essence.

3 Lightly beat the egg whites with a fork. Add the chocolate mixture and continue to beat well. Sift the flour over the mixture and fold in with the oat bran. Pour into the prepared tin.

4 Cook in the preheated oven for 40 minutes or until firm. Cool in the tin for 10 minutes, then turn out on to a wire rack. Cut into squares and lightly dust with icing sugar before serving.

SPLIT PEA AND COURGETTE SOUP

Rich and satisfying, this tasty and nutritious soup will warm a chilly winter's day.

INGREDIENTS

Serves 4

175g/6oz/1⅛ cups yellow split peas
1 medium onion, finely chopped
5ml/1 tsp sunflower oil
2 medium courgettes, finely diced
900ml/1½ pints/3¾ cups chicken stock
2.5ml/½ tsp ground turmeric
salt and black pepper

1 Place the split peas in a bowl, cover with cold water and leave to soak for several hours or overnight. Drain, rinse in cold water and drain again.

2 Cook the onion in the oil in a covered pan, shaking occasionally, until soft. Reserve a handful of diced courgettes and add the rest to the pan. Cook, stirring, for 2–3 minutes.

3 Add the stock and turmeric to the pan and bring to the boil. Reduce the heat, then cover and simmer for 30–40 minutes, or until the split peas are tender. Adjust the seasoning.

4 When the soup is almost ready, bring a large saucepan of water to the boil, add the reserved diced courgettes and cook for 1 minute, then drain and add to the soup before serving hot with warm crusty bread.

COOK'S TIP
For a quicker alternative, use split red lentils for this soup – they need no presoaking and cook very quickly. Adjust the amount of stock, if necessary.

NUTRITION NOTES

Per portion:

Energy	174Kcals/730kJ
Fat	2.14g
Saturated fat	0.54g
Cholesterol	0
Fibre	3.43g

COFFEE SPONGE DROPS

These are delicious on their own, but taste even better with a filling made by mixing low fat soft cheese with drained and chopped stem ginger.

INGREDIENTS

Makes 12
50g/2oz/½ cup plain flour
15ml/1 tbsp instant coffee powder
2 eggs
75g/3oz/6 tbsp caster sugar

For the filling
115g/4oz/½ cup low fat soft cheese
40g/1½oz/¼ cup chopped
    stem ginger

COOK'S TIP
As an alternative to stem ginger in the filling, try walnuts.

1 Preheat the oven to 190°C/375°F/ Gas 5. Line two baking sheets with non-stick baking paper. Make the filling by beating together the soft cheese and stem ginger. Chill until required. Sift the flour and instant coffee powder together.

2 Combine the eggs and caster sugar in a bowl. Beat with a hand-held electric whisk until thick and mousse-like. (When the whisk is lifted, a trail should remain on the surface of the mixture for at least 15 seconds.)

NUTRITION NOTES	
Per portion:	
Energy	69Kcals/290kJ
Fat	1.36g
Saturated Fat	0.50g
Cholesterol	33.33mg
Fibre	0.29g

3 Carefully add the sifted flour and coffee mixture and gently fold in with a metal spoon, being careful not to knock out any air.

4 Spoon the mixture into a piping bag fitted with a 1cm/½in plain nozzle. Pipe 4cm/1½in rounds on the baking sheets. Bake for 12 minutes. Cool on a wire rack, then sandwich together with the filling.

RED PEPPER SOUP WITH LIME

The beautiful rich red colour of this soup makes it a very attractive starter or light lunch. For a special dinner, toast some tiny croutons and serve sprinkled into the soup.

INGREDIENTS

Serves 4–6
4 red peppers, seeded and chopped
1 large onion, chopped
5ml/1 tsp olive oil
1 garlic clove, crushed
1 small red chilli, sliced
45ml/3 tbsp tomato purée
900ml/1½ pints/3¾ cups chicken stock
finely grated rind and juice of 1 lime
salt and black pepper
shreds of lime rind, to garnish

1 Cook the onion and peppers gently in the oil in a covered saucepan for about 5 minutes, shaking the pan occasionally, until softened.

2 Stir in the garlic, then add the chilli with the tomato purée. Stir in half the stock, then bring to the boil. Cover the pan and simmer for 10 minutes.

3 Cool slightly, then purée in a food processor or blender. Return to the pan, then add the remaining stock, the lime rind and juice, and seasoning.

4 Bring the soup back to the boil, then serve at once with a few strips of lime rind, scattered into each bowl.

NUTRITION NOTES	
Per portion:	
Energy	87Kcals/366kJ
Fat	1.57g
Saturated fat	0.12g
Cholesterol	0
Fibre	3.40g

APRICOT SPONGE BARS

These fingers are delicious at tea time – the apricots keep them moist for several days.

Makes 18
225g/8oz/2 cups self-raising flour
115g/4oz/½ cup soft light brown sugar
50g/2oz/½ cup semolina
175g/6oz/1 cup ready-to-eat dried
   apricots, chopped
30ml/2 tbsp clear honey
30ml/2 tbsp malt extract
2 eggs
60ml/4 tbsp skimmed milk
60ml/4 tbsp sunflower oil
a few drops of almond essence
30ml/2 tbsp flaked almonds

1 Preheat the oven to 160°C/325°F/ Gas 3. Lightly grease and then line an 18 x 28cm/7 x 11in baking tin.

2 Sift the flour into a bowl and mix in the sugar, semolina and apricots. Make a well in the centre and add the honey, malt extract, eggs, milk, oil and almond essence. Mix the ingredients together thoroughly until smooth.

3 Spoon the mixture into the tin, spreading it to the edges, then sprinkle over the flaked almonds.

4 Bake for 30–35 minutes, or until the centre springs back when lightly pressed. Remove from the tin and turn on to a wire rack to cool. Cut into 18 slices using a sharp knife.

COOK'S TIP
If you can't find pre-soaked apricots, just chop ordinary dried apricots soak them in boiling water for 1 hour, then drain and add to the mixture.

NUTRITION NOTES

Per portion:

Energy	153Kcals/641kJ
Fat	4.56g
Saturated Fat	0.61g
Cholesterol	21.5mg
Fibre	1.27g

Vegetable Minestrone

Serves 6–8

large pinch of saffron strands
1 onion, chopped
1 leek, sliced
1 stick celery, sliced
2 carrots, diced
2–3 garlic cloves, crushed
600ml/1 pint/2½ cups chicken stock
2 x 400g/14oz cans chopped tomatoes
50g/2oz/½ cup frozen peas
50g/2oz soup pasta (anellini)
5ml/1 tsp caster sugar
15ml/1 tbsp chopped fresh parsley
15ml/1 tbsp chopped fresh basil
salt and black pepper

1 Soak the pinch of saffron strands in 15ml/1 tbsp boiling water. Leave to stand for 10 minutes.

2 Meanwhile, put the prepared onion, leek, celery, carrots and garlic into a large pan. Add the chicken stock, bring to the boil, cover and simmer for about 10 minutes.

3 Add the canned tomatoes, the saffron with its liquid and the frozen peas. Bring back to the boil and add the soup pasta. Simmer for 10 minutes until tender.

> ### Cook's Tip
> Saffron strands aren't essential for this soup, but they give a wonderful delicate flavour, with the bonus of a lovely rich orange-yellow colour.

4 Season with sugar, salt and pepper to taste. Stir in the chopped herbs just before serving.

Nutrition Notes	
Per portion:	
Energy	87Kcals/367kJ
Fat	0.7g
Saturated Fat	0.1g
Cholesterol	0
Fibre	3.3g

MUSCOVADO MERINGUES

These light brown meringues are extremely low in fat and are delicious served on their own or sandwiched together with a fresh fruit and soft cheese filling.

INGREDIENTS

Makes about 20

115g/4oz/²⁄₃ cup light muscovado sugar
2 egg whites
5ml/1 tsp finely chopped walnuts

NUTRITION NOTES

Per portion:

Energy	30Kcals/124kJ
Fat	0.34g
Saturated Fat	0.04g
Cholesterol	0
Fibre	0.02g

1 Preheat the oven to 160°C/325°F/ Gas 3. Line two baking sheets with non-stick baking paper. Press the sugar through a metal sieve into a bowl.

2 Whisk the egg whites in a clean, dry bowl until very stiff and dry, then whisk in the sugar, about 15ml/1 tbsp at a time, until the meringue is very thick and glossy.

3 Spoon small mounds of the mixture on to the prepared baking sheets.

4 Sprinkle the meringues with the chopped walnuts. Bake for 30 minutes. Cool for 5 minutes on the baking sheets, then leave to cool on a wire rack.

COOK'S TIP
For a sophisticated filling, mix 115g/4oz/¹⁄₂ cup low fat soft cheese with 15ml/1 tbsp icing sugar. Chop 2 slices of fresh pineapple and add to the mixture. Use to sandwich the meringues together in pairs.

SWEETCORN CHOWDER WITH PASTA SHELLS

Smoked turkey rashers provide a tasty, low fat alternative to bacon in this hearty dish. If you prefer, omit the meat altogether and serve the soup as is.

INGREDIENTS

Serves 4

1 small green pepper
450g/1lb potatoes, peeled and diced
350g/12oz/2 cups canned or frozen
    sweetcorn
1 onion, chopped
1 celery stick, chopped
a bouquet garni (bay leaf, parsley stalks
    and thyme)
600ml/1 pint/2½ cups chicken stock
300ml/½ pint/1¼ cups skimmed milk
50g/2oz small pasta shells
oil, for frying
150g/5oz smoked turkey rashers, diced
salt and black pepper
bread sticks, to serve

1 Halve the green pepper, then remove the stalk and seeds. Cut the flesh into small dice, cover with boiling water and stand for 2 minutes. Drain and rinse.

NUTRITION NOTES	
Per portion:	
Energy	215Kcals/904kJ
Fat	1.6g
Saturated Fat	0.3g
Cholesterol	13mg
Fibre	2.8g

2 Put the potatoes into a saucepan with the sweetcorn, onion, celery, green pepper, bouquet garni and stock. Bring to the boil, cover and simmer for 20 minutes until tender.

3 Add the milk and season with salt and pepper. Process half of the soup in a food processor or blender and return to the pan with the pasta shells. Simmer for 10 minutes.

4 Fry the turkey rashers in a non-stick frying pan for 2–3 minutes. Stir into the soup. Season to taste and serve with bread sticks.

SNOWBALLS

These light and airy little mouthfuls make an excellent accompaniment to low fat yogurt ice cream.

INGREDIENTS

Makes about 20
2 egg whites
115g/4oz/¹/₂ cup caster sugar
15ml/1 tbsp cornflour, sifted
5ml/1 tsp white wine vinegar
1.5ml/¹/₄ tsp vanilla essence

1 Preheat the oven to 150C°/300°F/ Gas 2. Line two baking sheets with non-stick baking paper. Whisk the egg whites in a large grease-free bowl until very stiff, using an electric whisk.

2 Add the sugar, whisking until the meringue is very stiff. Whisk in the cornflour, vinegar and vanilla essence.

3 Drop teaspoonfuls of the mixture on to the baking sheets, shaping them into mounds, and bake for 30 minutes until crisp.

4 Remove from the oven and leave to cool on the baking sheet. When the snowballs are cold, remove them from the baking paper with a palette knife.

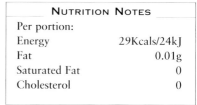

NUTRITION NOTES	
Per portion:	
Energy	29Kcals/24kJ
Fat	0.01g
Saturated Fat	0
Cholesterol	0

CARROT AND CORIANDER SOUP

Nearly all root vegetables make excellent soups as they purée well and have an earthy flavour which complements the sharper flavours of herbs and spices. Carrots are particularly versatile, and this simple soup is elegant in both flavour and appearance.

INGREDIENTS

Serves 6

10ml/2 tsp sunflower oil
1 onion, chopped
1 celery stick, sliced, plus 2–3 leafy celery tops
2 small potatoes, chopped
450g/1lb carrots, preferably young and tender, chopped
1 litre/1¾ pints/4 cups chicken stock
10–15ml/2–3 tsp ground coriander
15ml/1 tbsp chopped fresh coriander
200ml/7fl oz/1 cup semi-skimmed milk
salt and black pepper

1 Heat the oil in a large flameproof casserole or heavy-based saucepan and fry the onion over a gentle heat for 3–4 minutes until slightly softened but not browned. Add the celery and potato, cook for a few minutes, then add the carrot. Fry over a gentle heat for 3–4 minutes, stirring frequently, and then cover. Reduce the heat even further and cook for about 10 minutes. Shake the pan or stir occasionally so the vegetables do not stick to the base.

2 Add the stock, bring to the boil and then partially cover and simmer for a further 8–10 minutes until the carrot and potato are tender.

3 Remove 6–8 tiny celery leaves for a garnish and finely chop about 15ml/1 tbsp of the remaining celery tops. In a small saucepan, dry fry the ground coriander for about 1 minute, stirring constantly. Reduce the heat, add the chopped celery and fresh coriander and fry for about 1 minute. Set aside.

4 Process the soup in a food processor or blender and pour into a clean saucepan. Stir in the milk, coriander mixture and seasoning. Heat gently, taste and adjust the seasoning. Serve garnished with the reserved celery.

NUTRITION NOTES	
Per portion:	
Energy	76.5Kcals/320kJ
Fat	3.2g
Saturated fat	0.65g
Cholesterol	2.3mg
Fibre	2.2g

COOK'S TIP
For a more piquant flavour, add a little freshly squeezed lemon juice just before serving. The contrast between the orange-coloured soup and the green garnish is a feast for the eye as well as the tastebuds.

SPICED DATE AND WALNUT CAKE

A classic flavour combination, which makes a very easy low fat, high-fibre cake.

Makes 1 cake
300g/11oz/2½ cups wholemeal self-
  raising flour
10ml/2 tsp mixed spice
150g/5oz/¼ cup chopped dates
50g/2oz/½ cup chopped walnuts
60ml/4 tbsp sunflower oil
115g/4oz/½ cup dark muscovado sugar
300ml/½ pint/1¼ cups skimmed milk
walnut halves, to decorate

1 Preheat the oven to 180°C/350°F/ Gas 4. Grease and line a 900g/2 lb loaf tin with greaseproof paper.

2 Sift together the flour and spice, adding back any bran from the sieve. Stir in the dates and walnuts.

3 Mix the oil, sugar and milk, then stir evenly into the dry ingredients. Spoon into the prepared tin and arrange the walnut halves on top.

4 Bake the cake in the oven for about 45–50 minutes, or until golden brown and firm. Turn out the cake, remove the lining paper and leave to cool on a wire rack.

NUTRITION NOTES

Per cake:
Energy	2654Kcals/11146kJ
Fat	92.78g
Saturated fat	11.44g
Cholesterol	6mg
Fibre	35.1g

COOK'S TIP
Pecan nuts can be used in place of the walnuts in this cake.

CAULIFLOWER AND BEAN SOUP

The sweet, liquorice flavour of the fennel seeds gives a delicious edge to this hearty soup.

INGREDIENTS

Serves 6
10ml/2 tsp olive oil
1 garlic clove, crushed
1 onion, chopped
10ml/2 tsp fennel seeds
1 cauliflower, cut into small florets
2 x 400g/14oz cans flageolet beans, drained and rinsed
1.2 litres/2 pints/5 cups vegetable stock or water
salt and black pepper
chopped fresh parsley, to garnish
toasted slices of French bread, to serve

1 Heat the olive oil. Add the garlic, onion and fennel seeds and cook gently for 5 minutes or until the onion is softened.

2 Add the cauliflower, half of the beans and all the stock or water.

3 Bring to the boil. Reduce the heat and simmer for 10 minutes or until the cauliflower is tender.

NUTRITION NOTES	
Per portion:	
Energy	194.3Kcals/822.5kJ
Fat	3.41g
Saturated Fat	0.53g
Cholesterol	0
Fibre	7.85g

4 Pour the soup into a blender and blend until smooth. Stir in the remaining beans and season to taste. Reheat and pour into bowls. Sprinkle with chopped parsley and serve with toasted slices of French bread.

BANANA GINGER PARKIN

Parkin keeps well and really improves with keeping. Store it in a covered container for up to two months.

INGREDIENTS

Makes 1 cake
200g/7oz/1¼ cups plain flour
10ml/2 tsp bicarbonate of soda
10ml/2 tsp ground ginger
150g/5oz/1¼ cups medium oatmeal
60ml/4 tbsp dark muscovado sugar
75g/3oz/6 tbsp sunflower margarine
150g/5oz/⅔ cup golden syrup
1 egg, beaten
3 ripe bananas, mashed
75g/3oz/¼ cup icing sugar
stem ginger, to decorate

1 Preheat the oven to 160°C/325°F/ Gas 3. Grease and line an 18 x 28cm/7 x 11in cake tin.

2 Sift together the flour, bicarbonate of soda and ginger, then stir in the oatmeal. Melt the sugar, margarine and syrup in a saucepan, then stir into the flour mixture. Beat in the egg and mashed bananas.

3 Spoon into the tin and bake for about 1 hour, or until firm to the touch. Allow to cool in the tin, then turn out and cut into squares.

4 Sift the icing sugar into a bowl and stir in just enough water to make a smooth, runny icing. Drizzle the icing over each square and top with a piece of stem ginger, if you like.

> **COOK'S TIP**
> This is a nutritious, energy-giving cake that is a really good choice for packed lunches as it doesn't break up too easily.

NUTRITION NOTES

Per cake:

Energy	3320Kcals/13946kJ
Fat	83.65g
Saturated fat	16.34g
Cholesterol	197.75mg
Fibre	20.69g

BEETROOT AND APRICOT SWIRL

This soup is most attractive if you swirl together the two coloured mixtures, but if you prefer they can be mixed together to save on time and washing up.

Serves 4

*4 large cooked beetroot, roughly
    chopped
1 small onion, roughly chopped
600ml/1 pint/2½ cups chicken stock
200g/7oz/1 cup ready-to-eat dried
    apricots
250ml/8 fl oz/1 cup orange juice
salt and black pepper*

1 Place the beetroot and half the onion in a pan with the stock. Bring to the boil, then reduce the heat, cover and simmer for about 10 minutes. Purée in a food processor or blender.

2 Place the rest of the onion in a pan with the apricots and orange juice, cover and simmer gently for about 15 minutes, until tender. Purée in a food processor or blender.

3 Return the two mixtures to the saucepans and reheat. Season to taste with salt and pepper, then swirl them together in individual soup bowls for a marbled effect.

COOK'S TIP
The apricot mixture should be the same consistency as the beetroot mixture – if it is too thick, then add a little more orange juice.

──── NUTRITION NOTES ────

Per portion:
Energy	135Kcals/569kJ
Fat	0.51g
Saturated fat	0.01g
Cholesterol	0
Fibre	4.43g

PEAR AND SULTANA TEABREAD

This is an ideal teabread to make when pears are plentiful – an excellent use for windfalls.

INGREDIENTS

Serves 6–8

25g/1oz/¹/₄ cup rolled oats
50g/2oz/¹/₄ cup light muscovado sugar
30ml/2 tbsp pear or apple juice
30ml/2 tbsp sunflower oil
1 large or 2 small pears
115g/4oz/1 cup self-raising flour
115g/4oz/³/₄ cup sultanas
2.5ml/¹/₂ tsp baking powder
10ml/2 tsp mixed spice
1 egg

1 Preheat the oven to 180°C/350°F/ Gas 4. Grease and line a 450g/1lb loaf tin with non-stick baking paper. Put the oats in a bowl with the sugar, pour over the pear or apple juice and oil, mix well and leave to stand for 15 minutes.

2 Quarter, core and coarsely grate the pear(s). Add to the oat mixture with the flour, sultanas, baking powder, mixed spice and egg, then mix together thoroughly.

3 Spoon the mixture into the prepared loaf tin and level the top. Bake for 50–60 minutes or until a skewer inserted into the centre comes out clean.

COOK'S TIP
Health food shops sell concentrated pear and apple juice, ready for diluting as required.

4 Transfer the teabread on to a wire rack and peel off the lining paper. Leave to cool completely.

NUTRITION NOTES

Per portion:

Energy	200Kcals/814kJ
Fat	4.61g
Saturated Fat	0.79g
Cholesterol	27.50mg
Fibre	1.39g

THAI-STYLE SWEETCORN SOUP

This is a very quick and easy soup, made in minutes. If you are using frozen prawns, then defrost them first before adding to the soup.

INGREDIENTS

Serves 4

2.5ml/½ tsp sesame or sunflower oil
2 spring onions, thinly sliced
1 garlic clove, crushed
600ml/1 pint/2½ cups chicken stock
425g/15oz can cream-style sweetcorn
225g/8oz/1¼ cups cooked, peeled
  prawns
5ml/1 tsp green chilli paste or chilli
  sauce (optional)
salt and black pepper
fresh coriander leaves, to garnish

1 Heat the oil in a large heavy-based saucepan and sauté the onions and garlic over a medium heat for 1 minute, until softened, but not browned.

2 Stir in the chicken stock, cream-style sweetcorn, prawns and chilli paste or sauce, if using.

3 Bring the soup to the boil, stirring occasionally. Season to taste, then serve at once, sprinkled with fresh coriander leaves to garnish.

COOK'S TIP
If cream-style corn is not available, use ordinary canned sweetcorn, puréed in a food processor for a few seconds, until creamy yet with some texture left.

NUTRITION NOTES	
Per portion:	
Energy	202Kcals/848kJ
Fat	3.01g
Saturated fat	0.43g
Cholesterol	45.56mg
Fibre	1.6g

ANGEL CAKE

A delicious light cake to serve as a dessert for a special occasion.

INGREDIENTS

Serves 10

40g/1½oz/⅓ cup cornflour
40g/1½oz/⅓ cup plain flour
8 egg whites
225g/8oz/1 cup caster sugar, plus extra for sprinkling
5ml/1 tsp vanilla essence
90ml/6 tbsp orange-flavoured glacé icing, 4–6 physalis and a little icing sugar, to decorate

1 Preheat the oven to 180°C/350°F/Gas 4. Sift both flours on to a sheet of greaseproof paper.

2 Whisk the egg whites in a large, clean, dry bowl until very stiff, then gradually add the sugar and vanilla essence, whisking until the mixture is thick and glossy.

3 Gently fold in the flour mixture with a large metal spoon. Spoon into an ungreased 25cm/10in angel cake tin, smooth the surface and bake for about 45–50 minutes, until the cake springs back when lightly pressed.

COOK'S TIP
If you prefer, omit the glacé icing and physalis and simply dust the cake with a little icing sugar – it is delicious to serve as a coffee-time treat, and also makes the perfect accompaniment to vanilla yogurt ice cream for a dessert.

4 Sprinkle a piece of greaseproof paper with caster sugar and set an egg cup in the centre. Invert the cake tin over the paper, balancing it carefully on the egg cup. When cold, the cake will drop out of the tin. Transfer it to a plate, spoon over the glacé icing, arrange the physalis on top and then dust with icing sugar and serve.

NUTRITION NOTES

Per portion:

Energy	139Kcals/582kJ
Fat	0.08g
Saturated Fat	0.01g
Cholesterol	0
Fibre	0.13g

MELON, PINEAPPLE AND GRAPE COCKTAIL

A light, refreshing fruit salad, with no added sugar and virtually no fat, perfect for breakfast or brunch – or any time.

INGREDIENTS

Serves 4

½ melon
225g/8oz fresh pineapple or 225g/8oz
* can pineapple chunks in own juice*
225g/8oz seedless white grapes, halved
120ml/4fl oz/½ cup white grape juice
fresh mint leaves, to decorate (optional)

1 Remove the seeds from the melon half and use a melon baller to scoop out even-size balls.

COOK'S TIP
A melon is ready to eat when it smells sweet even through its thick skin. Use a firm-fleshed fruit, such as a Galia or honey-dew melon.

2 Using a sharp knife, cut the skin from the pineapple and discard. Cut the fruit into bite-size chunks.

3 Combine all the fruits in a glass serving dish and pour over the juice. If you are using canned pineapple, measure the drained juice and make it up to the required quantity with the grape juice.

4 If not serving immediately, cover and chill. Serve decorated with mint leaves, if liked.

NUTRITION NOTES

Per portion:

Energy	95Kcals/395kJ
Fat	0.5g
Saturated Fat	0
Cholesterol	0

IRISH WHISKEY CAKE

This moist rich fruit cake is drizzled with whiskey as soon as it comes out of the oven.

INGREDIENTS

Serves 12

115g/4oz/²⁄₃ cup glacé cherries
175g/6oz/1 cup dark muscovado sugar
115g/4oz/²⁄₃ cup sultanas
115g/4oz/²⁄₃ cup raisins
115g/4oz/½ cup currants
300ml/½ pint/1¼ cups cold tea
300g/10oz/2½ cups self-raising
   flour, sifted
1 egg
45ml/3 tbsp Irish whiskey

COOK'S TIP
If time is short, use hot tea and soak the fruit for just 2 hours.

1 Mix the cherries, sugar, dried fruit and tea in a large bowl. Leave to soak overnight until all the tea has been absorbed into the fruit.

NUTRITION NOTES

Per portion:	
Energy	265Kcals/1115kJ
Fat	0.88g
Saturated Fat	0.25g
Cholesterol	16mg
Fibre	1.48g

2 Preheat the oven to 180°C/350°F/ Gas 4. Grease and line a 1kg/2¼lb loaf tin. Add the flour, then the egg to the fruit mixture and beat thoroughly until well mixed.

3 Pour the mixture into the prepared tin and bake for 1½ hours or until a skewer inserted into the centre of the cake comes out clean.

4 Prick the top of the cake with a skewer and drizzle over the whiskey while the cake is still hot. Allow to stand for about 5 minutes, then remove from the tin and cool on a wire rack.

GUACAMOLE WITH CRUDITÉS

This fresh-tasting spicy dip is made using peas instead of the avocado pears that are traditionally associated with this dish. This version saves on both fat and calories, without compromising on taste.

INGREDIENTS

Serves 4–6

350g/12oz/2¼ cups frozen peas,
   defrosted
1 garlic clove, crushed
2 spring onions, chopped
5ml/1 tsp finely grated rind and juice of
   1 lime
2.5ml/½ tsp ground cumin
dash of Tabasco sauce
15ml/1 tbsp reduced fat mayonnaise
30ml/2 tbsp chopped fresh coriander
   or parsley
salt and black pepper
pinch of paprika and lime slices,
   to garnish

For the crudités

6 baby carrots
2 celery sticks
1 red-skinned eating apple
1 pear
15ml/1 tbsp lemon or lime juice
6 baby sweetcorn

2 Add the chopped coriander or parsley and process for a few more seconds. Spoon into a serving bowl, cover with clear film and chill in the fridge for 30 minutes, to let the flavours develop fully.

3 For the crudités, trim and peel the carrots. Halve the celery sticks lengthways and trim into sticks, the same length as the carrots. Quarter, core and thickly slice the apple and pear, then dip into the lemon or lime juice. Arrange with the baby sweetcorn on a platter.

NUTRITION NOTES

Per portion:
Energy	110Kcals/460kJ
Protein	6.22g
Fat	2.29g
Saturated Fat	0.49g
Fibre	6.73g

1 Put the peas, garlic clove, spring onions, lime rind and juice, cumin, Tabasco sauce, mayonnaise and salt and black pepper into a food processor or a blender for a few minutes and process until smooth.

COOK'S TIP
Serve the guacamole dip with warmed wholemeal pitta bread.

4 Sprinkle the paprika over the guacamole and garnish with twisted lime slices.

BANANA ORANGE LOAF

For the best banana flavour and a really good, moist texture, make sure the bananas are very ripe for this cake.

INGREDIENTS

Makes 1 loaf

90g/3½oz/¼ cup wholemeal plain flour
90g/3½oz/¼ cup plain flour
5ml/1 tsp baking powder
5ml/1 tsp ground mixed spice
45ml/3 tbsp flaked hazelnuts, toasted
2 large ripe bananas
1 egg
30ml/2 tbsp sunflower oil
30ml/2 tbsp clear honey
finely grated rind and juice 1 small orange
4 orange slices, halved
10ml/2 tsp icing sugar

1 Preheat the oven to 180°C/350°F/ Gas 4. Brush a 1 litre/1¾ pint/4 cup loaf tin with sunflower oil and line the base with non-stick baking paper.

2 Sift the flour with the baking powder and spice into a large bowl, adding any bran that is caught in the sieve. Stir the hazelnuts into the dry ingredients.

3 Peel and mash the bananas. Beat in the egg, oil, honey and the orange rind and juice. Stir evenly into the dry ingredients.

4 Spoon into the prepared tin and smooth the top. Bake for 40–45 minutes, or until firm and golden brown. Turn out and cool on a wire rack to cool.

5 Sprinkle the orange slices with the icing sugar and grill until golden. Use to decorate the cake.

> **COOK'S TIP**
> If you plan to keep the loaf for more than two or three days, omit the orange slices, brush with honey and sprinkle with flaked hazelnuts.

NUTRITION NOTES

Per cake:

Energy	1741Kcals/7314kJ
Fat	60.74g
Saturated fat	7.39g
Cholesterol	192.5mg
Fibre	19.72g

TZATZIKI

Tzatziki is a Greek cucumber salad dressed with yogurt, mint and garlic. It is typically served with grilled lamb and chicken, but is also good served with crudités.

INGREDIENTS

Serves 4
1 cucumber
5ml/1 tsp salt
45ml/3 tbsp finely chopped fresh mint, plus a few sprigs to garnish
1 garlic clove, crushed
5ml/1 tsp caster sugar
200ml/7fl oz reduced fat Greek-style yogurt
cucumber flower, to garnish (optional)

1 Peel the cucumber. Reserve a little of the cucumber to use as a garnish if you wish and cut the rest in half lengthways. Remove the seeds with a teaspoon and discard. Slice the cucumber thinly and combine with salt. Leave for approximately 15–20 minutes. Salt will soften the cucumber and draw out any bitter juices.

COOK'S TIP
If you want to prepare Tzatziki in a hurry, then leave out the method for salting cucumber at the end of step 1. The cucumber will have a more crunchy texture, and will be slightly less sweet.

2 Combine the mint, garlic, sugar and yogurt in a bowl, reserving a few sprigs of mint as decoration.

3 Rinse the cucumber in a sieve under cold running water to flush away the salt. Drain well and combine with the yogurt. Decorate with cucumber flower and/or mint. Serve cold.

NUTRITION NOTES

Per portion:	
Energy	41.5Kcals/174.5kJ
Fat	0.51g
Saturated Fat	0.25g
Cholesterol	2mg
Fibre	0.2g

CRANBERRY AND APPLE RING

Tangy cranberries add an unusual flavour to this low fat cake. It is best eaten very fresh.

INGREDIENTS

Makes 1 ring cake
225g/8oz/2 cups self-raising flour
5ml/1 tsp ground cinnamon
75g/3oz/½ cup light muscovado sugar
1 crisp eating apple, cored and diced
75g/3oz/¾ cup fresh or frozen
   cranberries
60ml/4 tbsp sunflower oil
150ml/¼ pint/⅔ cup apple juice
cranberry jelly and apple slices, to
   decorate

1 Preheat the oven to 180°C/350°F/ Gas 4. Lightly grease a 1 litre/1¼ pint/4 cup ring tin with oil.

2 Sift together the flour and ground cinnamon, then stir in the sugar.

3 Toss together the diced apple and cranberries. Stir into the dry ingredients, then add the oil and apple juice and beat well.

4 Spoon the mixture into the prepared ring tin and bake for about 35–40 minutes, or until the cake is firm to the touch. Turn out and leave to cool completely on a wire rack.

5 To serve, drizzle warmed cranberry jelly over the cake and decorate with apple slices.

COOK'S TIP
Fresh cranberries are available throughout the winter months and if you don't use them all at once, they can be frozen for up to a year.

NUTRITION NOTES

Per cake:
Energy   1616Kcals/6787kJ
Fat   47.34g
Saturated fat   6.14g
Cholesterol   0
Fibre   12.46g

CHILLI TOMATO SALSA

This universal dip is great served with absolutely anything and can be made up to 24 hours in advance.

INGREDIENTS

Serves 4

1 shallot, peeled and halved
2 garlic cloves, peeled
handful of fresh basil leaves
500g/1¼ lb ripe tomatoes
10ml/2 tsp olive oil
2 green chillies
salt and black pepper

1 Place the shallot and garlic in a food processor with the fresh basil. Whizz the shallot, garlic and basil until finely chopped.

2 Halve the tomatoes and add to the food processor. Pulse the machine until the mixture is well blended and coarsely chopped.

3 With the motor running, slowly pour in the olive oil. Add salt and pepper to taste.

NUTRITION NOTES	
Per portion:	
Energy	28Kcals/79kJ
Fat	0.47g
Saturated Fat	0.13g
Cholesterol	0
Fibre	1.45g

4 Halve the chillies lengthways and remove the seeds. Finely slice the chillies widthways into tiny strips and stir into the tomato salsa. Serve at room temperature.

COOK'S TIP
The salsa is best made in the summer when tomatoes are at their best. In winter, use a drained 400g/14oz can of plum tomatoes.

Eggless Christmas Cake

Makes 1 x 18cm/7in square cake
75g/3oz/⅔ cup sultanas
75g/3oz/⅔ cup raisins
75g/3oz/½ cup currants
75g/3oz/⅓ cup glacé cherries, halved
50g/2oz/¼ cup cut mixed peel
250ml/8 fl oz/1 cup apple juice
25g/1oz/¼ cup toasted hazelnuts
30ml/2 tbsp pumpkin seeds
2 pieces stem ginger in syrup, chopped
finely grated rind of 1 lemon
120ml/4 fl oz/½ cup skimmed milk
50ml/2 fl oz/¼ cup sunflower oil
225g/8oz/1¼ cups wholemeal self-
*   raising flour*
10ml/2 tsp mixed spice
45ml/3 tbsp brandy or dark rum
apricot jam, for brushing
glacé fruits, to decorate

1 Place the sultanas, raisins, currants, cherries and peel in a bowl and stir in the apple juice. Cover and leave to soak overnight.

2 Preheat the oven to 150°C/300°F/ Gas 2. Grease and line an 18cm/7in square cake tin.

3 Add the hazelnuts, pumpkin seeds, ginger and lemon rind to the soaked fruit. Stir in the milk and oil. Sift the flour and spice and stir into the mixture with the brandy or rum.

4 Spoon into the prepared tin and bake for about 1½ hours, or until the cake is golden brown and firm to the touch.

5 Turn out and cool on a wire rack. Brush with sieved apricot jam and decorate with glacé fruits.

NUTRITION NOTES	
Per cake:	
Energy	2702Kcals/11352kJ
Fat	73.61g
Saturated fat	10.69g
Cholesterol	2.4mg
Fibre	29.46g

MUSHROOM CROUSTADES

The rich mushroom flavour of this filling is heightened by the addition of Worcestershire sauce.

INGREDIENTS

Serves 2–4

1 short French stick, about 25cm/10in
10ml/2 tsp olive oil
250g/9oz open cup mushrooms, quartered
10ml/2 tsp Worcestershire sauce
10ml/2 tsp lemon juice
30ml/2 tbsp skimmed milk
30ml/2 tbsp snipped fresh chives
salt and black pepper
snipped fresh chives, to garnish

1 Preheat the oven to 200°C/400°F/ Gas 6. Cut the French bread in half lengthways. Cut a scoop out of the soft middle of each, leaving a thick border all the way round.

2 Brush the bread with oil, place on a baking sheet and bake for about 6–8 minutes, until golden and crisp.

3 Place the mushrooms in a small saucepan with the Worcestershire sauce, lemon juice and milk. Simmer for about 5 minutes, or until most of the liquid is evaporated.

4 Remove from the heat, then add the chives and seasoning. Spoon into the bread croustades and serve hot, garnished with snipped chives.

NUTRITION NOTES	
Per portion:	
Energy	324Kcals/1361kJ
Fat	6.4g
Saturated fat	1.27g
Cholesterol	0.3mg
Fibre	3.07g

CAKES AND BAKES

TOMATO PESTO TOASTIES

Ready-made pesto is high in fat but, as its flavour is so powerful, it can be used in very small amounts with good effect, as in these tasty toasties.

INGREDIENTS

Serves 2
2 thick slices crusty bread
45ml/3 tbsp skimmed milk soft cheese
  or low fat fromage frais
10ml/2 tsp red or green pesto
1 beef tomato
1 red onion
salt and black pepper

1 Toast the bread slices on a hot grill until golden brown on both sides turning once. Leave to cool.

2 Mix together the skimmed milk soft cheese and pesto in a small bowl until well blended, then spread thickly on to the toasted bread.

3 Cut the beef tomato and red onion, crossways, into thin slices using a large sharp knife.

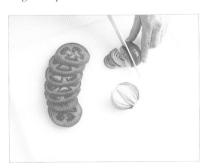

4 Arrange the slices, overlapping, on top of the toast and season with salt and pepper. Transfer the toasties to a grill rack and cook under a hot grill until heated through, then serve immediately.

COOK'S TIP
Almost any type of crusty bread can be used for this recipe, but Italian olive oil bread and French bread will give the best flavour.

NUTRITION NOTES

Per portion:	
Energy	177Kcals/741kJ
Fat	2.41g
Saturated fat	0.19g
Cholesterol	0.23mg
Fibre	2.2g

Tofu Berry Brulée

This is a lighter variation of a classic dessert, usually forbidden on a low fat diet, using tofu, which is low in fat and free from cholesterol. Use any soft fruits in season.

INGREDIENTS

Serves 4

300g/11oz packet silken tofu
45ml/3 tbsp icing sugar
225g/8oz/1½ cups red berry fruits, such as raspberries, strawberries and redcurrants
about 75ml/5 tbsp demerara sugar

1 Place the tofu and icing sugar in a food processor or blender and process until smooth.

2 Stir in the fruits and spoon into a 900ml/1½ pint/3¾ cup flameproof dish. Sprinkle the top with enough demerara sugar to cover evenly.

3 Place under a very hot grill until the sugar melts and caramelises. Chill before serving.

COOK'S TIP
Choose silken tofu rather than firm tofu as it gives a smoother texture in this type of dish. Firm tofu is better for cooking in chunks.

NUTRITION NOTES

Per portion:	
Energy	180Kcals/760kJ
Fat	3.01g
Saturated fat	0.41g
Cholesterol	0
Fibre	1.31g

CHEESE AND CHUTNEY TOASTIES

Quick cheese on toast can be made quite memorable with a few tasty additions. Serve these scrumptious toasties with a simple lettuce and cherry tomato salad.

INGREDIENTS

Serves 4

4 slices wholemeal bread, thickly sliced
85g/3½oz Cheddar cheese, grated
5ml/1 tsp dried thyme
30ml/2 tbsp chutney or relish
black pepper
salad, to serve

1 Toast the bread slices lightly on each side.

2 Mix the cheese and thyme together and season to taste with pepper.

NUTRITION NOTES

Per portion:

Energy	157.25Kcals/664.25kJ
Fat	4.24g
Saturated Fat	1.99g
Cholesterol	9.25mg
Fibre	2.41g

4 Return the toast to the grill and cook until the cheese is browned and bubbling. Cut each slice into halves, diagonally, and serve at once with salad.

COOK'S TIP
If you prefer, use a reduced fat hard cheese, such as mature Cheddar or Red Leicester, in place of the full fat Cheddar to cut both calories and fat.

---

3 Spread the chutney or relish on the toast and divide the cheese evenly between the four slices.

PLUM AND PORT SORBET

Rather a grown-up sorbet, this one, but you could use fresh, still red grape juice in place of the port if you prefer.

INGREDIENTS

Serves 4–6

1kg/2 lb ripe red plums, halved and stoned
75g/3oz/6 tbsp caster sugar
45ml/3 tbsp water
45ml/3 tbsp ruby port or red wine
crisp, sweet biscuits, to serve

1 Place the plums in a pan with the sugar and water. Stir over a gentle heat until the sugar is melted, then cover and simmer gently for about 5 minutes, until the fruit is soft.

2 Turn into a food processor and purée until smooth, then stir in the port. Cool completely, then tip into a freezer container and freeze until firm around the edges.

3 Spoon into the food processor and process until smooth. Return to the freezer and freeze until solid.

4 Allow to soften slightly at room temperature for 15–20 minutes before serving in scoops, with sweet biscuits.

NUTRITION NOTES	
Per portion:	
Energy	166Kcals/699kJ
Fat	0.25g
Saturated fat	0
Cholesterol	0
Fibre	3.75g

PARMA HAM AND PEPPER PIZZAS

The delicious flavours of these easy pizzas are hard to beat.

INGREDIENTS

Makes 4

½ loaf ciabatta bread
1 red pepper, roasted and peeled
1 yellow pepper, roasted and peeled
4 slices Parma ham, cut into
   thick strips
50g/2oz reduced fat mozzarella cheese
black pepper
tiny basil leaves, to garnish

NUTRITION NOTES

Per portion:
Energy	93Kcals/395kJ
Fat	3.25g
Saturated Fat	1.49g
Cholesterol	14mg
Fibre	1g

1 Cut the bread into four thick slices and toast until golden.

2 Cut the roasted peppers into thick strips and arrange on the toasted bread with the strips of Parma ham. Preheat the grill.

3 Thinly slice the mozzarella and arrange on top, then grind over plenty of black pepper. Grill for 2–3 minutes until the cheese is bubbling.

4 Scatter the basil leaves on top and serve immediately.

PINEAPPLE, ALLSPICE AND LIME

Fresh pineapple is easy to prepare and always looks very festive, so this dish is perfect for easy entertaining.

INGREDIENTS

Serves 4

1 ripe medium pineapple
1 lime
15ml/1 tbsp dark muscovado sugar
5ml/1 tsp ground allspice

1 Cut the pineapple lengthways into quarters and remove the core.

NUTRITION NOTES	
Per portion:	
Energy	39Kcals/163kJ
Fat	0.12g
Saturated Fat	0
Cholesterol	0
Fibre	0.68g

2 Loosen the fruit by sliding a knife between it and the skin. Cut the pineapple flesh into thick slices.

3 Remove a few shreds of rind from the lime and set aside, then squeeze out the juice.

4 Sprinkle the pineapple with the lime juice and rind, muscovado sugar and allspice. Serve immediately, or chill for up to 1 hour.

CHICKEN PITTAS WITH RED COLESLAW

Pittas are convenient for simple snacks and packed lunches and it's easy to pack in lots of fresh healthy ingredients.

INGREDIENTS

Serves 4

¼ red cabbage, finely shredded
1 small red onion, finely sliced
2 radishes, thinly sliced
1 red apple, peeled, cored and grated
15ml/1 tbsp lemon juice
45ml/3 tbsp low fat fromage frais
1 cooked chicken breast without skin, about 175g/6oz
4 large pittas or 8 small pittas
salt and black pepper
chopped fresh parsley, to garnish

1 Remove the tough central spine from the cabbage leaves, then finely shred the leaves using a large sharp knife. Place the shredded cabbage in a bowl and stir in the onion, radishes, apple and lemon juice.

2 Stir the fromage frais into the shredded cabbage mixture and season well with salt and pepper. Thinly slice the cooked chicken breast and stir into the shredded cabbage mixture until well coated in fromage frais.

3 Warm the pittas under a hot grill, then split them along one edge using a round-bladed knife. Spoon the filling into the pittas, then garnish with chopped fresh parsley.

COOK'S TIP
If the filled pittas need to be made more than an hour in advance, line the pitta breads with crisp lettuce leaves before adding the filling.

NUTRITION NOTES

Per portion:

Energy	232Kcals/976kJ
Fat	2.61g
Saturated fat	0.76g
Cholesterol	24.61mg
Fibre	2.97g

CRUNCHY FRUIT LAYER

INGREDIENTS

Serves 2

1 peach or nectarine

75g/3oz/1 cup crunchy toasted
   oat cereal

150ml/¼ pint/⅔ cup low fat
   natural yogurt

15ml/1 tbsp jam

15ml/1 tbsp fruit juice

NUTRITION NOTES

Per portion:

Energy	240Kcals/1005kJ
Fat	3g
Saturated Fat	1g
Cholesterol	3mg

1 Remove the stone from the peach or
nectarine and cut the fruit into
bite-size pieces with a sharp knife.

2 Divide the chopped fruit between
two tall glasses, reserving a few
pieces for decoration.

3 Sprinkle the oat cereal over the fruit
in an even layer, then top with the
low fat yogurt.

4 Stir the jam and the fruit juice
together in a jug, then drizzle the
mixture over the yogurt. Decorate with
the reserved peach or nectarine pieces
and serve at once.

GRANARY SLTs

A quick, tasty snack or easy packed lunch with a healthy combination – sardines, lettuce and tomatoes!

INGREDIENTS

Serves 2

2 small Granary bread rolls
120g/4¼oz can sardines in olive oil
4 crisp green lettuce leaves, such as
    Webbs
1 beef tomato, sliced
juice of ½ lemon
salt and black pepper

1 Slice the bread rolls in half cross-ways using a sharp knife. Drain off the oil from the sardines into a small bowl, then brush the cut surfaces of the rolls with a small amount of the oil.

2 Cut or break the sardines into small pieces, then fill each roll with a lettuce leaf, some sliced tomato and pieces of sardine, sprinkling the filling with a little lemon juice, and salt and pepper to taste.

3 Sandwich the rolls back together and press the lids down lightly with your hand. Serve at once.

NUTRITION NOTES

Per portion:

Energy	248Kcals/1042kJ
Fat	8.51g
Saturated fat	1.86g
Cholesterol	32.5mg
Fibre	3.01g

COOK'S TIP
If you prefer to use sardines in tomato sauce, spread the bread rolls thinly with low fat spread before adding the filling.

MANDARINS IN SYRUP

Mandarins, tangerines, clementines, mineolas; any of these lovely citrus fruits are suitable for this recipe.

INGREDIENTS

Serves 4

10 mandarin oranges
15ml/1 tbsp icing sugar
10ml/2 tsp orange-flower water
15ml/1 tbsp chopped pistachio nuts

1 Thinly pare a little of the rind from one mandarin and cut it into fine shreds for decoration. Squeeze the juice from two mandarins and set aside.

2 Peel the remaining fruit, removing as much of the white pith as possible. Arrange the peeled fruit whole in a wide dish.

3 Mix the mandarin juice, sugar and orange-flower water and pour it over the fruit. Cover the dish and chill for at least an hour.

4 Blanch the shreds of mandarin rind in boiling water for 30 seconds. Drain, leave to cool and then sprinkle them over the mandarins, with the pistachio nuts, to serve.

NUTRITION NOTES

Per portion:

Energy	53.25Kcals/223.5kJ
Fat	2.07g
Saturated Fat	0.28g
Cholesterol	0
Fibre	0.38g

COOK'S TIP
Mandarin oranges look very attractive if you leave them whole, but you may prefer to separate the segments.

CHINESE GARLIC MUSHROOMS

Tofu is high in protein and very low in fat, so it is a very useful food to keep handy for quick meals and snacks like this one.

INGREDIENTS

Serves 4

8 large open mushrooms
3 spring onions, sliced
1 garlic clove, crushed
30ml/2 tbsp oyster sauce
285g/10 oz packet marinated tofu, cut into small dice
200g/7oz can sweetcorn, drained
10ml/2 tsp sesame oil
salt and black pepper

1 Preheat the oven to 200°C/400°F/ Gas 6. Finely chop the mushroom stalks and mix with the spring onions, garlic and oyster sauce.

2 Stir in the diced marinated tofu and sweetcorn, season well with salt and pepper, then spoon the filling into the mushrooms.

3 Brush the edges of the mushrooms with the sesame oil. Arrange the stuffed mushrooms in a baking dish and bake for 12–15 minutes, until the mushrooms are just tender, then serve at once.

COOK'S TIP
If you prefer, omit the oyster sauce and use light soy sauce instead.

NUTRITION NOTES	
Per portion:	
Energy	137Kcals/575kJ
Fat	5.6g
Saturated fat	0.85g
Cholesterol	0
Fibre	1.96g

QUICK APRICOT WHIP

INGREDIENTS

Serves 4

400g/14oz can apricot halves in juice
15ml/1 tbsp Grand Marnier or brandy
175g/6oz/³/₄ cup low fat yogurt
30ml/2 tsp flaked almonds

NUTRITION NOTES	
Per portion:	
Energy	114Kcals/480kJ
Fat	4.6g
Saturated Fat	0.57g
Cholesterol	0
Fibre	1.45g

1 Drain the juice from the apricots and place the fruit and liqueur in a blender or food processor.

2 Process the apricots until they are completely smooth.

3 Put alternate spoonfuls of the fruit purée and yogurt into four tall glasses or glass dishes, swirling them together slightly to give a marbled effect.

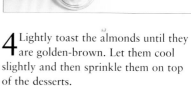

4 Lightly toast the almonds until they are golden-brown. Let them cool slightly and then sprinkle them on top of the desserts.

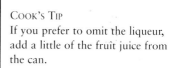

COOK'S TIP
If you prefer to omit the liqueur, add a little of the fruit juice from the can.

SURPRISE SCOTCH 'EGGS'

This reduced fat version of Scotch eggs is great for packed lunches or picnics. If half fat sausagemeat isn't available, buy half fat sausages or turkey sausages and remove the skins.

INGREDIENTS

Makes 3

75ml/5 tbsp chopped parsley and snipped chives, mixed
115g/4oz/½ cup skimmed milk soft cheese
450g/1 lb half fat sausagemeat
50g/2oz /½ cup rolled oats
salt and black pepper
mixed leaf and tomato salad, to serve

1 Preheat the oven to 200°C/400°F/ Gas 6. Mix together the herbs, cheese and seasonings, then roll into three even-sized balls.

2 Divide the sausagemeat into three and press each piece out to a round, about 1cm/½ in thick.

3 Wrap each cheese ball in a piece of sausagemeat, smoothing over all the joins to enclose the cheese completely. Spread out the rolled oats on a plate and roll the balls in the oats, using your hands to coat them evenly.

4 Place the balls on a baking sheet and bake for 30–35 minutes or until golden. Serve hot or cold, with a mixed leaf and tomato salad.

NUTRITION NOTES	
Per portion:	
Energy	352Kcals/1476kJ
Fat	15.94g
Saturated fat	0.29g
Cholesterol	66.38mg
Fibre	3.82g

ICED ORANGES

The ultimate fat-free treat – these delectable orange sorbets served in fruit shells were originally sold in the beach cafés in the south of France.

INGREDIENTS

Serves 8

150g/5oz/²/₃ cup granulated sugar
juice of 1 lemon
14 medium oranges
8 fresh bay leaves, to decorate

NUTRITION NOTES

Per portion:

Energy	139Kcals/593kJ
Fat	0.17g
Saturated Fat	0
Cholesterol	0
Fibre	3g

COOK'S TIP
Use crumpled kitchen paper to keep the shells upright.

1 Put the sugar in a heavy-based saucepan. Add half the lemon juice, then add 120ml/4fl oz/½ cup water. Cook over a low heat until the sugar has dissolved. Bring to the boil and boil for 2–3 minutes until the syrup is clear.

2 Slice the tops off eight of the oranges to make "hats". Scoop out the flesh of the oranges and reserve. Freeze the empty orange shells and "hats" until needed.

3 Grate the rind of the remaining oranges and add to the syrup. Squeeze the juice from the oranges, and from the reserved flesh. There should be 750ml/1¼ pints/3 cups. Squeeze another orange or add bought orange juice, if necessary.

4 Stir the orange juice and remaining lemon juice, with 90ml/6 tbsp water into the syrup. Taste, adding more lemon juice or sugar as desired. Pour the mixture into a shallow freezer container and freeze for 3 hours.

5 Turn the orange sorbet mixture into a bowl and whisk thoroughly to break up the ice crystals. Freeze for 4 hours more, until firm, but not solid.

6 Pack the mixture into the hollowed-out orange shells, mounding it up, and set the "hats" on top. Freeze the sorbet shells until ready to serve. Just before serving, push a skewer into the tops of the "hats" and push in a bay leaf, to decorate.

MUSSELS WITH THAI HERBS

Another simple dish to prepare.
The lemon grass adds a refreshing tang to the mussels.

INGREDIENTS

Serves 6

1kg/2¼ lb mussels, cleaned and beards
   removed
2 lemon grass stalks, finely chopped
4 shallots, chopped
4 kaffir lime leaves, roughly torn
2 red chillies, sliced
15ml/1 tbsp fish sauce
30ml/2 tbsp lime juice
2 spring onions, chopped, and
   coriander leaves, to garnish

1 Put all the ingredients, except the
spring onions and coriander, in a
large saucepan and stir thoroughly.

2 Cover and cook for 5–7 minutes,
shaking the saucepan occasionally,
until the mussels open. Discard any
mussels that do not open.

3 Transfer the cooked mussels to a
serving platter.

4 Garnish the mussels with chopped
spring onions and coriander leaves.
Serve immediately.

NUTRITION NOTES	
Per portion:	
Energy	56Kcals/238kJ
Fat	1.22g
Saturated Fat	0.16g
Cholesterol	0.32g
Fibre	27g

RHUBARB AND ORANGE WATER-ICE

Pretty pink rhubarb, with sweet oranges and honey – the perfect sweet ice.

INGREDIENTS

Serves 4

350g/12oz rhubarb
1 medium orange
15ml/1 tbsp clear honey
5ml/1 tsp/1 sachet powdered gelatine
orange slices, to decorate

COOK'S TIP
Most pink, forced rhubarb is naturally quite sweet, but if yours is not, you can add a little more honey, sugar or artificial sweetener to taste.

1 Trim the rhubarb and slice into 2.5cm/1in lengths. Put the pieces in a pan without adding water.

NUTRITION NOTES

Per portion:	
Energy	36Kcals/155kJ
Fat	0.12g
Saturated Fat	0
Cholesterol	0
Fibre	1.9g

2 Finely grate the rind from the orange and squeeze out the juice. Add about half the orange juice and all the grated rind to the rhubarb in the pan and allow to simmer until the rhubarb is just tender. Stir in the honey.

3 Heat the remaining orange juice and sprinkle in the gelatine to dissolve it. Stir into the rhubarb. Turn the whole mixture into a rigid freezer container and freeze it for about 2 hours until slushy.

4 Remove the mixture from the freezer and beat it well to break up the ice crystals. Return to the freezer and freeze again until firm. Allow the water-ice to soften slightly at room temperature before serving.

MEAT DISHES

MANGO AND GINGER CLOUDS

The sweet, perfumed flavour of ripe mango combines beautifully with ginger, and this low fat dessert makes the very most of them both.

INGREDIENTS

Serves 6
3 ripe mangoes
3 pieces stem ginger
45ml/3 tbsp stem ginger syrup
75g/3oz/¹/₂ cup silken tofu
3 egg whites
6 pistachio nuts, chopped

1 Cut the mangoes in half, remove the stones and peel. Roughly chop the mango flesh.

2 Put the chopped mango in a food processor bowl, with the ginger, syrup and tofu. Process the mixture until smooth and spoon into a mixing bowl.

3 Put the egg whites in a bowl and whisk them until they form soft peaks. Fold them lightly into the mango mixture.

4 Spoon the mixture into wide dishes or glasses and chill before serving, sprinkled with the chopped pistachios.

NUTRITION NOTES	
Per portion:	
Energy	112Kcals/472kJ
Fat	3.5g
Saturated Fat	0.52g
Cholesterol	0
Fibre	2.25g

COOK'S TIP
This dessert can be served lightly frozen. If you prefer not to use ginger, omit the ginger pieces and syrup and use 45ml/3 tbsp clear honey instead.

PORK AND CELERY POPOVERS

Lower in fat than they look, and a good way to make the meat go further, these little popovers will be popular with children.

INGREDIENTS

Serves 4

sunflower oil, for brushing
150g/5oz plain flour
1 egg white
250ml/8 fl oz/1 cup skimmed milk
120ml/4 fl oz/½ cup water
350g/12 oz lean minced pork
2 celery sticks, finely chopped
45ml/3 tbsp rolled oats
30ml/2 tbsp snipped chives
15ml/1 tbsp Worcestershire or brown sauce
salt and black pepper

1 Preheat the oven to 220°C/425°F/ Gas 7. Brush 12 deep patty tins with a very little oil.

2 Place the flour in a bowl and make a well in the centre. Add the egg white and milk and gradually beat in the flour. Gradually add the water, beating until smooth and bubbly.

3 Place the minced pork, celery, oats, chives, Worcestershire sauce and seasoning in a bowl and mix thoroughly. Mould the mixture into 12 small balls and place in the patty tins.

4 Cook for 10 minutes, remove from the oven and quickly pour the batter into the tins. Cook for a further 20–25 minutes, or until well risen and golden brown. Serve hot with thin gravy and fresh vegetables.

NUTRITION NOTES	
Per portion:	
Energy	344Kcals/1443kJ
Fat	9.09g
Saturated fat	2.7g
Cholesterol	61.62mg
Fibre	2.37g

MELON, GINGER AND GRAPEFRUIT

This pretty fruit combination is very light and refreshing for any summer meal.

INGREDIENTS

Serves 4

500g/1¼ lbs diced watermelon flesh
2 ruby or pink grapefruit
2 pieces stem ginger in syrup
30ml/2 tbsp stem ginger syrup

NUTRITION NOTES

Per portion:
Energy	76Kcals/324.5kJ
Fat	0.42g
Saturated Fat	0.125g
Cholesterol	0
Fibre	0.77g

1 Remove any seeds from the watermelon and discard. Cut the fruit into bite-size chunks. Set aside.

2 Using a small sharp knife, cut away all the peel and white pith from the grapefruits and carefully lift out the segments, catching any juice in a bowl.

3 Finely chop the stem ginger and put in a serving bowl with the melon cubes and grapefruit segments, also adding the juice.

4 Spoon over the ginger syrup and toss the fruits lightly to mix evenly. Chill before serving.

> **COOK'S TIP**
> Take care to toss the fruits gently – grapefruit segments will break up easily and the appearance of the dish will be spoiled.

BEEF AND MUSHROOM BURGERS

It's worth making your own burgers to cut down on fat – in these the meat is extended with mushrooms for extra fibre.

INGREDIENTS

Serves 4

1 small onion, chopped
150g/5oz/2 cups small cup mushrooms
450g/1 lb lean minced beef
50g/2oz/1 cup fresh wholemeal bread-
  crumbs
5ml/1 tsp dried mixed herbs
15ml/1 tbsp tomato purée
flour, for shaping
salt and black pepper

1 Place the onion and mushrooms in a food processor and process until finely chopped. Add the beef, bread-crumbs, herbs, tomato purée and seasonings. Process for a few seconds, until the mixture binds together but still has some texture.

2 Divide the mixture into 8–10 pieces, then press into burger shapes using lightly floured hands.

3 Cook the burgers in a non-stick frying pan, or under a hot grill for 12-15 minutes, turning once, until evenly cooked. Serve with relish and salad, in burger buns or pitta bread.

COOK'S TIP
The mixture is quite soft, so handle carefully and use a fish slice for turning to prevent the burgers from breaking up during cooking.

NUTRITION NOTES

Per portion	
Energy	196Kcals/822kJ
Fat	5.9g
Saturated fat	2.21g
Cholesterol	66.37mg
Fibre	1.60g

APPLE FOAM WITH BLACKBERRIES

Any seasonal soft fruit can be used for this if blackberries are not available.

INGREDIENTS

Serves 4
225g/8oz blackberries
150ml/¼ pint/⅔ cup apple juice
5ml/1 tsp powdered gelatine
15ml/1 tbsp clear honey
2 egg whites

1 Place the blackberries in a pan with 60ml/4 tbsp of the apple juice and heat gently until the fruit is soft. Remove from the heat, cool and chill.

2 Sprinkle the gelatine over the remaining apple juice in a small pan and stir over a low heat until dissolved. Stir in the honey.

3 Whisk the egg whites until they hold stiff peaks. Continue whisking hard and pour in the hot gelatine mixture gradually, until well mixed.

4 Quickly spoon the foam into rough mounds on individual plates. Chill. Serve with the blackberries and juice spooned around.

COOK'S TIP
Make sure that you dissolve the gelatine over a very low heat. It must not boil, or it will lose its setting ability.

NUTRITION NOTES

Per portion:

Energy	49Kcals/206kJ
Fat	0.15g
Saturated fat	0
Cholesterol	0
Fibre	1.74g

COUNTRY PORK WITH PARSLEY COBBLER

This hearty casserole is a complete main course in one pot.

INGREDIENTS

Serves 4

450g/1 lb boneless pork shoulder, diced
1 small swede, diced
2 carrots, sliced
2 parsnips, sliced
2 leeks, sliced
2 celery sticks, sliced
750ml/1¼ pint/3⅔ cups boiling beef stock
30ml/2 tbsp tomato purée
30ml/2 tbsp chopped fresh parsley
50g/2oz/¼ cup pearl barley
celery salt and black pepper

For the topping
150g/5oz/1 cup plain flour
5ml/1 tsp baking powder
90ml/6 tbsp low fat fromage frais
45ml/3 tbsp chopped fresh parsley

1 Preheat the oven to 180°C/350°F/ Gas 4. Fry the pork without fat, in a non-stick pan until lightly browned.

2 Add the vegetables to the pan and stir over a medium heat until lightly coloured. Tip into a large casserole dish, then stir in the stock, tomato purée, parsley and pearl barley.

3 Season with celery salt and pepper, then cover and place in the oven for about 1–1¼ hours, until the pork and vegetables are tender.

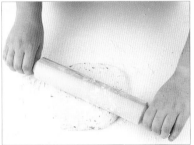

4 For the topping, sift the flour and baking powder with seasoning, then stir in the fromage frais and parsley with enough cold water to mix to a soft dough. Roll out to about 1cm/½ in thickness and cut into 12–16 triangles.

5 Remove the casserole from the oven and raise the temperature to 220°C/ 425°F/Gas 7.

6 Arrange the triangles over the casserole, overlapping. Bake for 15–20 minutes, until well risen and golden.

NUTRITION NOTES

Per portion:

Energy	461Kcals/1936kJ
Fat	10.55g
Saturated fat	3.02g
Cholesterol	77.85mg
Fibre	9.44g

APRICOT MOUSSE

This light, fluffy dessert can be made with any dried fruits instead of apricots – try dried peaches, prunes or apples.

INGREDIENTS

Serves 4

300g/10oz/1½ cups ready-to-eat dried apricots
300ml/½ pint/1¼ cups fresh orange juice
200g/7oz/⅞ cup low fat fromage frais
2 egg whites
mint sprigs, to decorate

1 Place the apricots in a saucepan with the orange juice and heat gently until boiling. Cover and simmer gently for 3 minutes.

2 Cool slightly. Place in a food processor or blender and process until smooth. Stir in the fromage frais.

3 Whisk the egg whites until stiff enough to hold soft peaks, then fold into the apricot mixture.

4 Spoon into four stemmed glasses or one large serving dish. Chill before serving.

COOK'S TIP
To make a speedier fool-type dish, omit the egg whites and simply swirl together the apricot mixture and fromage frais.

NUTRITION NOTES

Per portion:

Energy	180Kcals/757kJ
Fat	0.63g
Saturated fat	0.06g
Cholesterol	0.5mg
Fibre	4.8g

THAI BEEF SALAD

A hearty salad of beef, laced with a chilli and lime dressing.

INGREDIENTS

Serves 6

75g/3oz lean sirloin steaks
1 red onion, finely sliced
1/2 cucumber, finely sliced
   into matchsticks
1 lemon grass stalk, finely chopped
30ml/2 tbsp chopped spring onions
juice of 2 limes
15–30ml/1–2 tbsp fish sauce
2–4 red chillies, finely sliced, to garnish
fresh coriander, Chinese mustard cress
   and mint leaves, to garnish

NUTRITION NOTES

Per portion:

Energy	101Kcals/424kJ
Fat	3.8g
Saturated Fat	1.7g
Cholesterol	33.4mg
Fibre	0.28g

COOK'S TIP
Rump or fillet steaks would work just as well in this recipe. Choose good-quality lean steaks and remove and discard any visible fat.

1 Grill the sirloin steaks until they are medium-rare, then allow to rest for 10–15 minutes.

2 When cool, thinly slice the beef and put the slices in a large bowl.

3 Add the sliced onion, cucumber matchsticks and lemon grass.

4 Add the spring onions. Toss and season with lime juice and fish sauce. Serve at room temperature or chilled, garnished with the chillies, coriander, mustard cress and mint.

RASPBERRY PASSION FRUIT SWIRLS

If passion fruit is not available, this simple dessert can be made with raspberries alone.

INGREDIENTS

Serves 4

300g/11oz/2½ cups raspberries
2 passion fruit
400g/14oz/1¾ cups low fat fromage frais
30ml/2 tbsp caster sugar
raspberries and sprigs of mint, to decorate

1 Mash the raspberries in a small bowl with a fork until the juice runs. Scoop out the passion fruit pulp into a separate bowl with the fromage frais and sugar and mix well.

2 Spoon alternate spoonfuls of the raspberry pulp and the fromage frais mixture into stemmed glasses or one large serving dish, stirring lightly to create a swirled effect.

3 Decorate each dessert with a whole raspberry and a sprig of fresh mint. Serve chilled.

COOK'S TIP
Over-ripe, slightly soft fruit can also be used in this recipe. Use frozen raspberries when fresh are not available, but thaw first.

NUTRITION NOTES

Per portion:

Energy	110Kcals/462kJ
Fat	0.47g
Saturated fat	0.13g
Cholesterol	1mg
Fibre	2.12g

BEEF STRIPS WITH ORANGE AND GINGER

Stir-frying is one of the best ways to cook with the minimum of fat. It's also one of the quickest ways to cook, but you do need to choose tender meat.

INGREDIENTS

Serves 4

450g/1 lb lean beef rump, fillet or sirloin, cut into thin strips
finely grated rind and juice of 1 orange
15ml/1 tbsp light soy sauce
5ml/1 tsp cornflour
2.5cm/1in piece root ginger, finely chopped
10ml/2 tsp sesame oil
1 large carrot, cut into thin strips
2 spring onions, thinly sliced

1 Place the beef strips in a bowl and sprinkle over the orange rind and juice. If possible, leave to marinate for at least 30 minutes.

2 Drain the liquid from the meat and set aside, then mix the meat with the soy sauce, cornflour and ginger.

NUTRITION NOTES	
Per portion:	
Energy	175Kcals/730kJ
Fat	6.81g
Saturated fat	2.31g
Cholesterol	66.37mg
Fibre	0.67g

3 Heat the oil in a wok or large frying pan and add the beef. Stir-fry for 1 minute until lightly coloured, then add the carrot and stir-fry for a further 2–3 minutes.

4 Stir in the spring onions and reserved liquid, then cook, stirring, until boiling and thickened. Serve hot with rice noodles or plain boiled rice.

FRUITED RICE RING

This unusual rice pudding looks beautiful turned out of a ring mould but if you prefer, stir the fruit into the rice and serve in individual dishes.

INGREDIENTS

Serves 4

65g/2½oz/5 tbsp short grain rice
900ml/1½ pint/3¾ cups semi-skimmed milk
1 cinnamon stick
175g/6oz/1½ cups dried fruit salad
175ml/6 fl oz/¾ cup orange juice
45ml/3 tbsp caster sugar
finely grated rind of 1 small orange

1 Place the rice, milk and cinnamon stick in a large pan and bring to the boil. Cover and simmer, stirring occasionally, for about 1½ hours, until no free liquid remains.

2 Meanwhile, place the fruit and orange juice in a pan and bring to the boil. Cover and simmer very gently for about 1 hour, until tender and no free liquid remains.

3 Remove the cinnamon stick from the rice and stir in the sugar and orange rind.

4 Tip the fruit into the base of a lightly oiled 1.5 litre/2½ pint/6 cup ring mould. Spoon the rice over, smoothing down firmly. Chill.

5 Run a knife around the edge of the mould and turn out the rice carefully on to a serving plate.

NUTRITION NOTES	
Per portion:	
Energy	343Kcals/1440kJ
Fat	4.4g
Saturated fat	2.26g
Cholesterol	15.75mg
Fibre	1.07g

LAMB PIE WITH MUSTARD THATCH

A pleasant change from a classic shepherd's pie – healthier, too.

INGREDIENTS

Serves 4

750g/1½ lb old potatoes, diced
30ml/2 tbsp skimmed milk
15ml/1 tbsp wholegrain or French
  mustard
450g/1 lb lean minced lamb
1 onion, chopped
2 celery sticks, sliced
2 carrots, diced
150ml/¼ pint/⅔ cup beef stock
60ml/4 tbsp rolled oats
15ml/1 tbsp Worcestershire sauce
30ml/2 tbsp fresh chopped rosemary,
  or 10ml/2 tsp dried
salt and black pepper

1 Cook the potatoes in boiling, lightly salted water until tender. Drain and mash until smooth, then stir in the milk and mustard. Meanwhile, preheat the oven to 200°C/400°F/Gas 6.

2 Break up the lamb with a fork and fry without fat in a non-stick pan until lightly browned. Add the onion, celery and carrots to the pan and cook for 2–3 minutes, stirring.

3 Stir in the stock and rolled oats. Bring to the boil, then add the Worcestershire sauce and rosemary and season to taste with salt and pepper.

4 Turn the meat mixture into a 1.8 litre/3 pint/7 cup ovenproof dish and spread over the potato topping evenly, swirling with the edge of a knife. Bake for 30–35 minutes, or until golden. Serve hot with fresh vegetables.

NUTRITION NOTES	
Per portion:	
Energy	422Kcals/1770kJ
Fat	12.41g
Saturated fat	5.04g
Cholesterol	89.03mg
Fibre	5.07g

COLD
DESSERTS

SAUSAGE BEANPOT WITH DUMPLINGS

Sausages needn't be totally banned on a low fat diet, but choose them carefully. If you are unable to find a reduced-fat variety, choose turkey sausages instead, and always drain off any fat during cooking.

INGREDIENTS

Serves 4

450g/1 lb half-fat sausages
1 medium onion, thinly sliced
1 green pepper, seeded and diced
1 small red chilli, sliced, or 2.5ml/½ tsp chilli sauce
400g/14oz can chopped tomatoes
250ml/8 fl oz/1 cup beef stock
425g/15oz can red kidney beans, drained
salt and black pepper

For the dumplings
275g/10oz/2½ cups plain flour
10ml/2 tsp baking powder
225g/8oz/1 cup cottage cheese

1 Fry the sausages without fat in a non-stick pan until brown. Add the onion and pepper. Stir in the chilli, tomatoes and stock; bring to the boil.

2 Cover and simmer gently for 15–2 minutes, then add the beans and bring to the boil.

3 To make the dumplings, sift the flour and baking powder together and add enough water to mix to a firm dough. Roll out thinly and stamp out 16–18 rounds using a 7.5cm/3in cutter.

4 Place a small spoonful of cottage cheese on each round and bring the edges of the dough together, pinching to enclose. Arrange the dumplings over the sausages in the pan, cover the pan and simmer for 10–12 minutes, until the dumplings are well risen. Serve hot.

NUTRITION NOTES

Per portion:

Energy	574Kcals/2409kJ
Fat	13.09g
Saturated fat	0.15g
Cholesterol	52.31mg
Fibre	9.59g

GINGERBREAD UPSIDE DOWN PUDDING

A proper pudding goes down well on a cold winter's day. This one is quite quick to make and looks very impressive.

INGREDIENTS

Serves 4–6
sunflower oil, for brushing
15ml/1 tbsp soft brown sugar
4 medium peaches, halved and stoned,
   or canned peach halves
8 walnut halves

For the base
130g/4½oz/½ cup wholemeal flour
2.5ml/½ tsp bicarbonate of soda
7.5ml/1½ tsp ground ginger
5ml/1 tsp ground cinnamon
115g/4oz/½ cup molasses sugar
1 egg
120ml/4 fl oz/½ cup skimmed milk
50ml/2 fl oz/¼ cup sunflower oil

1 Preheat the oven to 175°C/350°F/ Gas 4. For the topping, brush the base and sides of a 23cm/9in round springform cake tin with oil. Sprinkle the sugar over the base.

2 Arrange the peaches cut-side down in the tin with a walnut half in each.

3 For the base, sift together the flour, bicarbonate of soda, ginger and cinnamon, then stir in the sugar. Beat together the egg, milk and oil, then mix into the dry ingredients until smooth.

4 Pour the mixture evenly over the peaches and bake for 35–40 minutes, until firm to the touch. Turn out onto a serving plate. Serve hot with yogurt or custard.

NUTRITION NOTES	
Per portion:	
Energy	432Kcals/1812kJ
Fat	16.54g
Saturated fat	2.27g
Cholesterol	48.72mg
Fibre	4.79g

RAGOÛT OF VEAL

If you are looking for a low-calorie dish to treat yourself – or some guests – then this is perfect, and quick, too.

INGREDIENTS

Serves 4

375g/12oz veal fillet or loin
10ml/2 tsp olive oil
10–12 tiny onions, kept whole
1 yellow pepper, seeded and cut
   into eighths
1 orange or red pepper, seeded and
   cut into eighths
3 tomatoes, peeled
   and quartered
4 fresh basil sprigs
30ml/2 tbsp dry martini or sherry
salt and black pepper

NUTRITION NOTES

Per portion:
Energy	158Kcals/665.5kJ
Fat	4.97g
Saturated Fat	1.14g
Cholesterol	63mg
Fibre	2.5g

1 Trim off any fat and cut the veal into cubes. Heat the oil in a frying pan and gently stir-fry the veal and onions until browned.

2 After a couple of minutes, add the peppers and tomatoes. Continue stir-frying for another 4–5 minutes.

3 Add half the basil leaves, roughly chopped (keep some for garnish), the martini or sherry, and seasoning. Cook, stirring frequently, for another 10 minutes, or until the meat is tender.

4 Sprinkle with the remaining basil leaves and serve hot.

> COOK'S TIP
> Lean beef or pork fillet may be used instead of veal, if you prefer. Shallots can replace the onions.

CRUNCHY GOOSEBERRY CRUMBLE

Gooseberries are perfect for traditional family puddings like this one. When they are out of season, other fruits such as apple, plums or rhubarb could be used instead.

INGREDIENTS

Serves 4

500g/1¼ lb/5 cups gooseberries
50g/2oz/4 tbsp caster sugar
75g/3oz/1 cup rolled oats
75g/3oz/¼ cup wholemeal flour
60ml/4 tbsp sunflower oil
50g/2oz/4 tbsp demerara sugar
30ml/2 tbsp chopped walnuts
natural yogurt or custard, to serve

1 Preheat the oven to 200°C/400°F/ Gas 6. Place the gooseberries in a pan with the caster sugar. Cover the pan and cook over a low heat for 10 minutes, until the gooseberries are just tender. Tip into an ovenproof dish.

2 To make the crumble, place the oats, flour and oil in a bowl and stir with a fork until evenly mixed.

3 Stir in the demerara sugar and walnuts, then spread evenly over the gooseberries. Bake for 25–30 minutes, or until golden and bubbling. Serve hot with yogurt, or custard made with skimmed milk.

COOK'S TIP
The best cooking gooseberries are the early small, firm green ones.

NUTRITION NOTES

Per portion:

Energy	422Kcals/1770kJ
Fat	18.5g
Saturated fat	2.32g
Cholesterol	0
Fibre	5.12g

POULTRY

SOUFFLÉED ORANGE SEMOLINA

Semolina has a poor reputation as a rather dull, sloppy pudding, but cooked like this you would hardly recognise it.

INGREDIENTS

Serves 4

50g/2oz/¼ cup semolina
600ml/1 pint/2½ cups semi-skimmed milk
30ml/2 tbsp light muscovado sugar
1 large orange
1 egg white

1 Preheat the oven to 200°C/400°F/ Gas 6. Place the semolina in a non-stick pan with the milk and sugar. Stir over a moderate heat until thickened and smooth. Remove from the heat.

2 Grate a few long shreds of orange rind from the orange and save for decoration. Finely grate the remaining rind. Cut all the peel and white pith from the orange and remove the segments. Stir into the semolina with the orange rind.

3 Whisk the egg white until stiff but not dry, then fold lightly and evenly into the mixture. Spoon into a 1 litre/ 1¾ pint/4 cup ovenproof dish and bake for 15–20 minutes, until risen and golden brown. Serve immediately.

COOK'S TIP
When using the rind of citrus fruit, scrub the fruit thoroughly before use, or buy unwaxed fruit.

NUTRITION NOTES

Per portion:

Energy	158Kcals/665kJ
Fat	2.67g
Saturated fat	1.54g
Cholesterol	10.5mg
Fibre	0.86g

TURKEY PASTITSIO

A traditional Greek pastitsio is a rich, high fat dish made with beef mince, but this lighter version is just as tasty.

INGREDIENTS

Serves 4–6
450g/1 lb lean minced turkey
1 large onion, finely chopped
60ml/4 tbsp tomato purée
250ml/8 fl oz/1 cup red wine or stock
5ml/1 tsp ground cinnamon
300g/11oz/2½ cups macaroni
300ml/½ pint/1¼ cups skimmed milk
25g/1oz/2 tbsp sunflower margarine
25g/1oz/3 tbsp plain flour
5ml/1 tsp grated nutmeg
2 tomatoes, sliced
60ml/4 tbsp wholemeal breadcrumbs
salt and black pepper
green salad, to serve

1 Preheat the oven to 220°C/425°F/ Gas 7. Fry the turkey and onion in a non-stick pan without fat, stirring until lightly browned.

2 Stir in the tomato purée, red wine or stock and cinnamon. Season, then cover and simmer for 5 minutes.

3 Cook the macaroni in boiling, salted water until just tender, then drain. Layer with the meat mixture in a wide ovenproof dish.

4 Place the milk, margarine and flour in a saucepan and whisk over a moderate heat until thickened and smooth. Add the nutmeg, and salt and pepper to taste.

5 Pour the sauce evenly over the pasta and meat. Arrange the tomato slices on top and sprinkle lines of breadcrumbs over the surface.

6 Bake for 30–35 minutes, or until golden brown and bubbling. Serve hot with a green salad.

NUTRITION NOTES	
Per portion:	
Energy	566Kcals/2382kJ
Fat	8.97g
Saturated fat	1.76g
Cholesterol	57.06mg
Fibre	4.86g

FRUITY BREAD PUDDING

A delicious family favourite pud from grandmother's day, with a lighter, healthier touch.

INGREDIENTS

Serves 4

75g/3oz/½ cup mixed dried fruit
150ml/¼ pint/⅔ cup apple juice
115g/4oz stale brown or white bread, diced
5ml/1 tsp mixed spice
1 large banana, sliced
150ml/¼ pint/⅔ cup skimmed milk
15ml/1 tbsp demerara sugar
natural low fat yogurt, to serve

1 Preheat the oven to 200°C/400°F/ Gas 6. Place the dried fruit in a small pan with the apple juice and bring to the boil.

2 Remove the pan from the heat and stir in the bread, spice and banana Spoon the mixture into a shallow 1.2 litre/2 pint/5 cup ovenproof dish and pour over the milk.

3 Sprinkle with demerara sugar and bake for 25–30 minutes, until firm and golden brown. Serve hot or cold with natural yogurt.

COOK'S TIP
Different types of bread will absorb varying amounts of liquid, so you may need to adjust the amount of milk to allow for this.

NUTRITION NOTES

Per portion:	
Energy	190Kcals/800kJ
Fat	0.89g
Saturated fat	0.21g
Cholesterol	0.75mg
Fibre	1.8g

TUSCAN CHICKEN

This simple peasant casserole has all the flavours of traditional Tuscan ingredients. The wine can be replaced by chicken stock.

INGREDIENTS

Serves 4

8 chicken thighs, skinned
5ml/1 tsp olive oil
1 medium onion, sliced thinly
2 red peppers, seeded and sliced
1 garlic clove, crushed
300ml/ ½ pint/1¼ cups passata
150ml/¼ pint/⅔ cup dry white wine
large sprig fresh oregano, or 5ml/1 tsp
  dried oregano
400g/14oz can cannelini beans, drained
45ml/3 tbsp fresh breadcrumbs
salt and black pepper

1 Fry the chicken in the oil in a non-stick or heavy pan until golden brown. Remove and keep hot. Add the onion and peppers to the pan and gently sauté until softened, but not brown. Stir in the garlic.

2 Add the chicken, passata, wine and oregano. Season well, bring to the boil then cover the pan tightly.

NUTRITION NOTES

Per portion:

Energy	248Kcals/1045kJ
Fat	7.53g
Saturated fat	2.06g
Cholesterol	73mg
Fibre	4.03g

3 Lower the heat and simmer gently, stirring occasionally for 30–35 minutes or until the chicken is tender and the juices run clear, not pink, when pierced with the point of a knife.

4 Stir in the cannelini beans and simmer for a further 5 minutes until heated through. Sprinkle with the breadcrumbs and cook under a hot grill until golden brown.

FILO CHIFFON PIE

Filo pastry is low in fat and is very easy to use. Keep a pack in the freezer, ready to make impressive desserts like this one.

INGREDIENTS

Serves 6
500g/1¼lb rhubarb
5ml/1 tsp mixed spice
finely grated rind and juice of 1 orange
15ml/1 tbsp granulated sugar
15g/½oz/1 tbsp butter
3 filo pastry sheets

1 Preheat the oven to 200°C/400°F/ Gas 6. Chop the rhubarb into 2.5cm/1in pieces and put them in a bowl.

2 Add the mixed spice, orange rind and juice and sugar. Tip the rhubarb into a 1 litre/1¾ pint/4 cup pie dish.

NUTRITION NOTES

Per portion:
Energy	71Kcals/299kJ
Fat	2.5g
Saturated Fat	1.41g
Cholesterol	5.74mg
Fibre	1.48g

3 Melt the butter and brush it over the pastry. Lift the pastry on to the pie dish, butter-side up, and crumple it up decoratively to cover the pie.

> VARIATION
> Other fruit can be used in this pie – just prepare depending on type.

4 Put the dish on a baking sheet and bake for 20 minutes, until golden brown. Reduce the heat to 180°C/350°F/ Gas 4 and bake for a further 10–15 minutes, until the rhubarb is tender.

TURKEY SPIRALS

These little spirals may look difficult, but they're very simple to make, and a very good way to pep up plain turkey.

INGREDIENTS

Serves 4

4 thinly sliced turkey breast steaks, about 90g/3½oz each
20ml/4 tsp tomato purée
15g/½oz/½ cup large basil leaves
1 garlic clove, crushed
15ml/1 tbsp skimmed milk
30ml/2 tbsp wholemeal flour
salt and black pepper
passata or fresh tomato sauce and pasta with fresh basil, to serve

1 Place the turkey steaks on a board. If too thick, flatten them slightly by beating with a rolling pin.

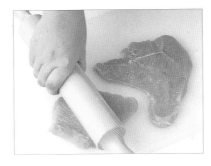

2 Spread each turkey breast steak with tomato purée, then top with a few leaves of basil, a little crushed garlic, and salt and pepper.

3 Roll up firmly around the filling and secure with a cocktail stick. Brush with milk and sprinkle with flour to coat lightly.

4 Place the spirals on a foil-lined grill-pan. Cook under a medium-hot grill for 15–20 minutes, turning them occasionally, until thoroughly cooked. Serve hot, sliced with a spoonful or two of passata or fresh tomato sauce and pasta, sprinkled with fresh basil.

COOK'S TIP
When flattening the turkey steaks with a rolling pin, place them between two sheets of cling film.

NUTRITION NOTES

Per portion:

Energy	123Kcals/518kJ
Fat	1.21g
Saturated fat	0.36g
Cholesterol	44.17mg
Fibre	0.87g

BLUEBERRY AND ORANGE CRÊPE BASKETS

Impress your guests with these pretty, fruit-filled crêpes. When blueberries are out of season, replace them with other soft fruit, such as raspberries.

INGREDIENTS

Serves 6
150g/5oz/1¼ cups plain flour
pinch of salt
2 egg whites
200ml/7fl oz/⅞ cup skimmed milk
150ml/¼ pint/⅔ cup orange juice
oil, for frying
yogurt or light crème fraîche, to serve

For the filling
4 medium oranges
225g/8oz/2 cups blueberries

1 Preheat the oven to 200°C/400°F/ Gas 6. To make the pancakes, sift the flour and salt into a bowl. Make a well in the centre and add the egg whites, milk and orange juice. Whisk hard, until all the liquid has been incorporated and the batter is smooth and bubbly.

2 Lightly grease a heavy or non-stick pancake pan and heat it until it is very hot. Pour in just enough batter to cover the base of the pan, swirling it to cover the pan evenly.

3 Cook until the pancake has set and is golden, then turn it to cook the other side. Remove the pancake to a sheet of kitchen paper. Cook the remaining batter to make 6–8 pancakes.

4 Place six small ovenproof bowls or moulds on a baking sheet and lay the pancakes over these. Bake them in the oven for about 10 minutes, until they are crisp and set into shape. Lift the 'baskets' off the moulds.

5 Pare a thin piece of orange rind from one orange and cut it into fine strips. Blanch the strips in boiling water for 30 seconds, rinse them in cold water and set them aside. Cut all the peel and white pith from the oranges.

6 Divide the oranges into segments, catching the juice, combine with the blueberries and warm them gently. Spoon the fruit into the baskets and scatter the rind over the top. Serve with yogurt or light crème fraîche.

COOK'S TIP
Don't fill the pancake baskets until you're ready to serve them, because they will absorb the fruit juice and begin to soften.

NUTRITION NOTES

Per portion:
Energy	157.3Kcals/668.3kJ
Fat	2.20g
Saturated Fat	0.23g
Cholesterol	0.66mg
Fibre	2.87g

CARIBBEAN CHICKEN KEBABS

These kebabs have a rich, sunshine Caribbean flavour and the marinade keeps them moist without the need for oil. Serve with a colourful salad and rice.

INGREDIENTS

Serves 4

500g/1¼ lb boneless chicken breasts, skinned
finely grated rind of 1 lime
30ml/2 tbsp lime juice
15ml/1 tbsp rum or sherry
15ml/1 tbsp light muscovado sugar
5ml/1 tsp ground cinnamon
2 mangoes, peeled and cubed
rice and salad, to serve

1 Cut the chicken into bite-sized chunks and place in a bowl with the lime rind and juice, rum, sugar and cinnamon. Toss well, cover and leave to stand for 1 hour.

2 Save the juices and thread the chicken on to four wooden skewers, alternating with the mango cubes.

3 Cook the skewers under a hot grill or barbecue for 8–10 minutes, turning occasionally and basting with the juices, until the chicken is tender and golden brown. Serve at once with rice and salad.

COOK'S TIP
The rum or sherry adds a lovely rich flavour, but it is optional so can be omitted if you prefer to make the dish more economical.

NUTRITION NOTES

Per portion:
Energy	218Kcals/918kJ
Fat	4.17g
Saturated fat	1.33g
Cholesterol	53.75mg
Fibre	2.26g

APPLE AND BLACKCURRANT PANCAKES

These pancakes are made with a wholewheat batter and are filled with a delicious fruit mixture.

INGREDIENTS

Makes 10

115g/4oz/1 cup plain wholemeal flour
300ml/½ pint/1¼ cups skimmed milk
1 egg, beaten
15ml/1 tbsp sunflower oil, plus extra
  for greasing
half fat crème fraîche, to serve
  (optional)
toasted nuts or sesame seeds, for
  sprinkling (optional)

For the filling

450g/1lb cooking apples
225g/8oz blackcurrants
30–45ml/2–3 tbsp water
30ml/2 tbsp demerara sugar

1 To make the pancake batter, put the flour in a mixing bowl and make a well in the centre.

2 Add a little of the milk with the egg and the oil. Beat the flour into the liquid, then gradually beat in the rest of the milk, keeping the batter smooth and free from lumps. Cover the batter and chill while you prepare the filling.

COOK'S TIP
If you wish, substitute other combinations of fruit for apples and blackcurrants.

3 Quarter, peel and core the apples. Slice them into a pan and add the blackcurrants and water. Cook over a gentle heat for 10–15 minutes until the fruit is soft. Stir in enough demerara sugar to sweeten.

NUTRITION NOTES	
Per portion:	
Energy	120Kcals/505kJ
Fat	3g
Saturated Fat	0.5g
Cholesterol	25mg

4 Lightly grease a non-stick pan with just a smear of oil. Heat the pan, pour in about 30ml/2 tbsp of the batter, swirl it around and cook for about 1 minute. Flip the pancake over with a palette knife and cook the other side. Put on a sheet of kitchen paper and keep hot while cooking the remaining pancakes.

5 Fill the pancakes with the apple and blackcurrant mixture and roll them up. Serve with a dollop of crème fraîche, if using, and sprinkle with nuts or sesame seeds, if liked.

OAT-CRUSTED CHICKEN WITH SAGE

Oats make a good coating for savoury foods, and offer a good way to add extra fibre.

INGREDIENTS

Serves 4

45ml/3 tbsp skimmed milk
10ml/2 tsp English mustard
40g/1½ oz/½ cup rolled oats
45ml/3 tbsp chopped sage leaves
8 chicken thighs or drumsticks, skinned
115g/4oz/½ cup low fat fromage frais
5ml/1 tsp wholegrain mustard
salt and black pepper
fresh sage leaves, to garnish

1 Preheat the oven to 200°C/400°F/ Gas 6. Mix together the milk and English mustard.

2 Mix the oats with 30ml/2 tbsp of the sage and the seasoning on a plate. Brush the chicken with the milk and press into the oats to coat evenly.

3 Place the chicken on a baking sheet and bake for about 40 minutes, or until the juices run clear, not pink, when pierced through the thickest part.

4 Meanwhile, mix together the low fat fromage frais, mustard, remaining sage and seasoning, then serve with the chicken. Garnish the chicken with fresh sage and serve hot or cold.

COOK'S TIP
If fresh sage is not available, choose another fresh herb such as thyme or parsley, instead of using a dried alternative.

NUTRITION NOTES

Per portion:

Energy	214Kcals/898kJ
Fat	6.57g
Saturated fat	1.81g
Cholesterol	64.64mg
Fibre	0.74g

BAKED APPLES IN HONEY AND LEMON

A classic mix of flavours in a healthy, traditional family pudding. Serve warm, with skimmed-milk custard or low fat frozen yogurt.

INGREDIENTS

Serves 4
4 medium cooking apples
15ml/1 tbsp clear honey
grated rind and juice of 1 lemon
15ml/1 tbsp low fat spread
skimmed-milk custard, to serve

1 Preheat the oven to 180°C/350°F/ Gas 4. Remove the cores from the apples, leaving them whole.

NUTRITION NOTES

Per portion:
Energy	61Kcals/259.5kJ
Fat	1.62g
Saturated Fat	0.42g
Cholesterol	0.25mg

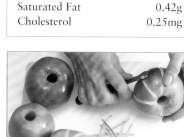

2 With a cannelle or sharp knife, cut lines through the apple skin at intervals. Put the apples in an oven-proof dish.

3 Mix together the honey, lemon rind, juice and low fat spread.

4 Spoon the mixture into the apples and cover the dish with foil or a lid. Bake for 40–45 minutes, or until the apples are tender. Serve with skimmed-milk custard.

CHICKEN IN CREAMY ORANGE SAUCE

This sauce is deceptively creamy – in fact it is made with low fat fromage frais, which is virtually fat-free. The brandy adds a richer flavour, but is optional – omit it if you prefer and use orange juice alone.

INGREDIENTS

Serves 4

8 chicken thighs or drumsticks, skinned
45ml/3 tbsp brandy
300ml/½ pint/1¼ cups orange juice
3 spring onions, chopped
10ml/2 tsp cornflour
90ml/6 tbsp low fat fromage frais
salt and black pepper

1 Fry the chicken pieces without fat in a non-stick or heavy pan, turning until evenly browned.

2 Stir in the brandy, orange juice and spring onions. Bring to the boil, then cover and simmer for 15 minutes, or until the chicken is tender and the juices run clear, not pink, when pierced.

3 Blend the cornflour with a little water then mix into the fromage frais. Stir this into the sauce and stir over a moderate heat until boiling.

4 Adjust the seasoning and serve with boiled rice or pasta and green salad.

COOK'S TIP
Cornflour stabilises the fromage frais and helps prevent it curdling.

NUTRITION NOTES	
Per portion:	
Energy	227Kcals/951kJ
Fat	6.77g
Saturated fat	2.23g
Cholesterol	87.83mg
Fibre	0.17g

SULTANA AND COUSCOUS PUDDING

Most couscous on the market now is the pre-cooked variety, which needs only the minimum of cooking, but check the packet instructions first to make sure. Serve hot, with yogurt or skimmed-milk custard.

INGREDIENTS

Serves 4
50g/2oz/¹⁄₃ cup sultanas
475ml/16fl oz/2 cups apple juice
90g/3¹⁄₂oz/1 cup couscous
2.5ml/¹⁄₂ tsp mixed spice

1 Lightly grease four 250ml/8fl oz/ 1 cup pudding basins or one 1 litre/1¾ pint/4 cup pudding basin. Put the sultanas and apple juice in a pan.

2 Bring the apple juice to the boil, then cover the pan and leave to simmer gently for 2–3 minutes to plump up the fruit. Using a slotted spoon, lift out about half the fruit and put it in the bottom of the basin(s).

3 Add the couscous and mixed spice to the pan and bring back to the boil, stirring. Cover and leave over a low heat for 8–10 minutes, or until the liquid has been absorbed.

NUTRITION NOTES	
Per portion:	
Energy	130.5Kcals/555kJ
Fat	0.40g
Saturated Fat	0
Cholesterol	0
Fibre	0.25g

4 Spoon the couscous into the basin(s), spread it level, then cover the basin(s) tightly with foil. Put the basin(s) in a steamer over boiling water, cover and steam for about 30 minutes. Run a knife around the edges, turn the puddings out carefully and serve.

> **COOK'S TIP**
> As an alternative, use chopped ready-to-eat dried apricots or pears, in place of the sultanas. Use unsweetened pineapple or orange juice in place of the apple juice.

BARBECUED CHICKEN

Serves 4 or 8

8 small chicken pieces
2 limes, cut into wedges, 2 red chillies,
finely sliced, and 2 lemon grass
stalks, to garnish
rice, to serve

For the marinade

2 lemon grass stalks, chopped
2.5cm/1in piece fresh root ginger
6 garlic cloves
4 shallots
¹/₂ bunch coriander roots
15ml/1 tbsp palm sugar
120ml/4fl oz/¹/₂ cup coconut milk
30ml/2 tbsp fish sauce
30ml/2 tbsp soy sauce

COOK'S TIP

Don't eat the skin of the chicken –
it's only left on to keep the flesh
moist during cooking. Coconut
milk makes a good base for a
marinade or sauce, as it is low in
calories and fat.

NUTRITION NOTES

Per portion (for 8):

Energy	106Kcals/449kJ
Fat	2.05g
Saturated Fat	1.10g
Cholesterol	1.10mg
Fibre	109g

1 To make the marinade, put all the
ingredients into a food processor
and process until smooth.

2 Put the chicken pieces in a dish and
pour over the marinade. Leave in a
cool place to marinate for at least
4 hours or overnight.

3 Preheat the oven to 200°C/400°F/
Gas 6. Put the chicken pieces on a
rack on a baking tray. Brush with
marinade and bake in the oven for
about 20–30 minutes or until the
chicken is cooked and golden brown.
Turn the pieces over halfway through
and brush with more marinade.

4 Garnish with lime wedges, finely
sliced red chillies and lemon grass
stalks. Serve with rice.

Strawberry and Apple Crumble

A high-fibre, healthier version of the classic apple crumble. Raspberries can be used instead of strawberries, either fresh or frozen.

INGREDIENTS

Serves 4
450g/1lb cooking apples
150g/5oz/1¼ cups strawberries
30ml/2 tbsp granulated sugar
2.5ml/½ tsp ground cinnamon
30ml/2 tbsp orange juice
custard or yogurt, to serve

For the crumble
45ml/3 tbsp plain wholemeal flour
50g/2oz/⅔ cup porridge oats
25g/1oz/⅛ cup low fat spread

1 Preheat the oven to 180°C/350°F/ Gas 4. Peel, core and slice the apples. Halve the strawberries.

NUTRITION NOTES

Per portion:	
Energy	182.3Kcals/785kJ
Fat	4g
Saturated Fat	0.73g
Cholesterol	0.5mg
Fibre	3.87g

2 Toss together the apples, straw-berries, sugar, cinnamon and orange juice. Tip into a 1.2 litre/ 2 pint/5 cup ovenproof dish, or four individual dishes.

3 Combine the flour and oats in a bowl and mix in the low fat spread with a fork.

4 Sprinkle the crumble evenly over the fruit. Bake for 40–45 minutes (20–25 minutes for individual dishes), until golden brown and bubbling. Serve warm with custard or yogurt.

CHICKEN, CARROT AND LEEK PARCELS

These intriguing parcels may sound a bit fiddly for everyday eating, but actually they take very little time, and you can freeze them ready to cook from frozen when needed.

INGREDIENTS

Serves 4

4 chicken fillets or skinless, boneless
   breast portions
2 small leeks, sliced
2 carrots, grated
2 stoned black olives, chopped
1 garlic clove, crushed
4 anchovy fillets, halved lengthways
salt and black pepper
black olives and herb sprigs, to garnish

1 Preheat the oven to 200°C/400°F/ Gas 6. Season the chicken well.

2 Cut out four sheets of lightly greased greaseproof paper about 23cm/9in square. Divide the leeks equally among them. Put a piece of chicken on top of each.

3 Mix the carrots, olives and garlic together. Season lightly and place on top of the chicken portions. Top each with two of the anchovy fillets.

4 Carefully wrap up each parcel, making sure the paper folds are sealed. Bake the parcels for 20 minutes and serve hot, in the paper, garnished with black olives and herb sprigs.

NUTRITION NOTES	
Per portion:	
Energy	154Kcals/651kJ
Fat	2.37g
Saturated Fat	0.45g
Cholesterol	78.75mg
Fibre	2.1g

COOK'S TIP
Skinless, boneless chicken is low in fat and is an excellent source of protein. Small, skinless turkey breast fillets also work well in this recipe and make a tasty change.

SPICED PEARS IN CIDER

Any variety of pear can be used for cooking, but it is best to choose firm pears for this recipe, or they will break up easily – Conference are a good choice.

INGREDIENTS

Serves 4
4 medium firm pears
250ml/8 fl oz/1 cup dry cider
thinly pared strip of lemon rind
1 cinnamon stick
30ml/2 tbsp light muscovado sugar
5ml/1 tsp arrowroot
ground cinnamon, to sprinkle

1 Peel the pears thinly, leaving them whole with the stalks on. Place in a pan with the cider, lemon rind and cinnamon. Cover and simmer gently, turning the pears occasionally for 15–20 minutes, or until tender.

2 Lift out the pears. Boil the syrup, uncovered to reduce by about half. Remove the lemon rind and cinnamon stick, then stir in the sugar.

3 Mix the arrowroot with 15ml/1 tbsp cold water in a small bowl until smooth, then stir into the syrup. Bring to the boil and stir over the heat until thickened and clear.

4 Pour the sauce over the pears and sprinkle with ground cinnamon. Leave to cool slightly, then serve warm with low fat fromage frais.

COOK'S TIP
Whole pears look very impressive, but if you prefer, they can be halved and cored before cooking. This will shorten the cooking time slightly.

NUTRITION NOTES

Per portion:	
Energy	102Kcals/428kJ
Fat	0.18g
Saturated fat	0.01g
Cholesterol	0
Fibre	1.65g

THAI CHICKEN AND VEGETABLE STIR-FRY

INGREDIENTS

Serves 4

1 piece lemon grass (or the rind of
   ½ lemon)
1cm/½in piece fresh root ginger
1 large garlic clove
30ml/2 tbsp sunflower oil
275g/10oz lean chicken,
   thinly sliced
½ red pepper, seeded and
   sliced
½ green pepper, seeded and sliced
4 spring onions, chopped
2 medium carrots, cut into matchsticks
115g/4oz fine green beans
25g/1oz peanuts, lightly crushed
30 ml/2 tbsp oyster sauce
pinch of sugar
salt and black pepper
coriander leaves, to garnish

NUTRITION NOTES	
Per portion:	
Energy	106Kcals/449kJ
Fat	2.05g
Saturated Fat	1.10g
Cholesterol	1.10mg
Fibre	109g

1 Thinly slice the lemon grass or lemon rind. Peel and chop the ginger and garlic. Heat the oil in a frying pan over a high heat. Add the lemon grass or lemon rind, ginger and garlic, and stir-fry for 30 seconds until brown.

2 Add the chicken and stir-fry for 2 minutes. Then add all the vegetables and stir-fry for 4–5 minutes, until the chicken is cooked and the vegetables are almost cooked.

3 Finally, stir in the peanuts, oyster sauce, sugar and seasoning to taste. Stir-fry for another minute to blend the flavours. Serve at once, sprinkled with the coriander leaves and accompanied by rice.

COOK'S TIP
Make this quick supper dish a little hotter by adding more fresh root ginger, if liked.

BANANA, MAPLE AND LIME PANCAKES

Pancakes are a treat any day of the week, and they can be made in advance and stored in the freezer for convenience.

INGREDIENTS

Serves 4
115g/4oz/1 cup plain flour
1 egg white
250ml/8 fl oz/1 cup skimmed milk
50ml/2 fl oz/¼ cup cold water
sunflower oil, for frying

For the filling
4 bananas, sliced
45ml/3 tbsp maple syrup or golden syrup
30ml/2 tbsp lime juice
strips of lime rind, to decorate

1 Beat together the flour, egg white, milk and water until smooth and bubbly. Chill until needed.

2 Heat a small amount of oil in a non-stick frying pan and pour in enough batter just to coat the base. Swirl it around the pan to coat evenly.

3 Cook until golden, then toss or turn and cook the other side. Place on a plate, cover with foil and keep hot while making the remaining pancakes.

4 To make the filling, place the bananas, syrup and lime juice in a pan and simmer gently for 1 minute. Spoon into the pancakes and fold into quarters. Sprinkle with shreds of lime rind to decorate. Serve hot, with yogurt or low fat fromage frais.

COOK'S TIP
Pancakes freeze well. To store for later use, interleave them with non-stick baking paper, overwrap and freeze for up to 3 months.

NUTRITION NOTES

Per portion:
Energy	282Kcals/1185kJ
Fat	2.79g
Saturated fat	0.47g
Cholesterol	1.25mg
Fibre	2.12g

FRAGRANT CHICKEN CURRY

In this dish, the mildly spiced sauce is thickened using lentils rather than the traditional onions fried in ghee.

INGREDIENTS

Serves 4–6

75g/3oz/¹/₂ cup red lentils
30ml/2 tbsp mild curry powder
10ml/2 tsp ground coriander
5ml/1 tsp cumin seeds
475ml/16fl oz/2 cups vegetable stock
8 chicken thighs, skinned
225g/8oz fresh shredded spinach, or
    frozen, thawed and well drained
15ml/1 tbsp chopped fresh coriander
salt and black pepper
sprigs of fresh coriander, to garnish
white or brown basmati rice and grilled
    poppadums, to serve

1 Rinse the lentils under cold running water. Put in a large, heavy-based saucepan with the curry powder, ground coriander, cumin seeds and stock.

2 Bring to the boil, then lower the heat. Cover and simmer gently for 10 minutes.

COOK'S TIP
Lentils are an excellent source of fibre, and add colour and texture.

3 Add the chicken and spinach. Replace the cover and simmer gently for a further 40 minutes, or until the chicken has cooked.

4 Stir in the chopped coriander and season to taste. Serve garnished with fresh coriander and accompanied by the rice and grilled poppadums.

HOT
PUDDINGS

FISH AND SEAFOOD

CACHUMBAR

Cachumbar is a salad relish most commonly served with Indian curries. There are many versions; this one will leave your mouth feeling cool and fresh·after a spicy meal.

INGREDIENTS

Serves 4

3 ripe tomatoes
2 chopped spring onions
1.5ml/¼ tsp caster sugar
salt
45ml/3 tbsp chopped fresh coriander

NUTRITION NOTES

Per portion:

Energy	9.5Kcals/73.5kJ
Fat	0.23g
Saturated Fat	0.07g
Cholesterol	0
Fibre	0.87g

1 Remove the tough cores from the bottom of the tomatoes with a small sharp-pointed knife.

> **COOK'S TIP**
> Cachumbar also makes a fine accompaniment to fresh crab, lobster and shellfish.

2 Halve the tomatoes, remove the seeds and dice the flesh.

3 Combine the tomatoes with the spring onions, sugar, salt and chopped coriander. Serve at room temperature.

HOKI BALLS IN TOMATO SAUCE

This quick meal is a good choice for young children, as you can guarantee no bones. If you like, add a dash of chilli sauce.

INGREDIENTS

Serves 4

450g/1 lb hoki or other white fish fillets, skinned
60ml/4 tbsp fresh wholemeal bread-crumbs
30ml/2 tbsp snipped chives or spring onion
400g/14oz can chopped tomatoes
50g/2oz/¼ cup button mushrooms, sliced
salt and black pepper

1 Cut the fish fillets into large chunks and place in a food processor. Add the wholemeal breadcrumbs, chives or spring onion. Season to taste with salt and pepper and process until the fish is finely chopped, but still has some texture left.

2 Divide the fish mixture into about 16 even-sized pieces, then mould them into balls with your hands.

3 Place the tomatoes and mushrooms in a wide saucepan and cook over a medium heat until boiling. Add the fish balls, cover and simmer for about 10 minutes, until cooked. Serve hot.

COOK'S TIP
Hoki is a good choice for this dish but if it's not available, use cod, haddock or whiting instead.

NUTRITION NOTES	
Per portion:	
Energy	138Kcals/580kJ
Fat	1.38g
Saturated fat	0.24g
Cholesterol	51.75mg
Fibre	1.89g

PRAWN NOODLE SALAD

A light, refreshing salad with all the tangy flavour of the sea. Instead of prawns, try squid, scallops, mussels or crab.

INGREDIENTS

Serves 4

115g/4oz cellophane noodles, soaked in hot water until soft
16 cooked prawns, peeled
1 small red pepper, seeded and cut into strips
½ cucumber, cut into strips
1 tomato, cut into strips
2 shallots, finely sliced
salt and black pepper
coriander leaves, to garnish

For the dressing

15ml/1 tbsp rice vinegar
30ml/2 tbsp fish sauce
30ml/2 tbsp fresh lime juice
pinch of salt
2.5ml/½ tsp grated fresh root ginger
1 lemon grass stalk, finely chopped
1 red chilli, seeded and finely sliced
30ml/2 tbsp roughly chopped mint
a few sprigs of tarragon, roughly chopped
15ml/1 tbsp snipped chives

1 Make the dressing by combining all the ingredients in a small bowl or jug; whisk well.

2 Drain the noodles, then plunge them in a saucepan of boiling water for 1 minute. Drain, rinse under cold running water and drain again well.

3 In a large bowl, combine the noodles with the prawns, red pepper, cucumber, tomato and shallots. Lightly season with salt and pepper, then toss with the dressing.

4 Spoon the noodles on to individual plates. Garnish with a few coriander leaves and serve at once.

NUTRITION NOTES

Per portion:

Energy	164.5Kcals/697kJ
Fat	2.9g
Saturated Fat	0.79g
Cholesterol	121mg
Fibre	1.86g

COOK'S TIP
Prawns are available ready-cooked and often shelled. To cook prawns, boil them for 5 minutes. Leave them to cool in the cooking liquid, then gently pull off the tail shell and twist off the head.

TUNA AND CORN FISH CAKES

These economical little tuna fish cakes are quick to make. Either use fresh mashed potatoes, or make a storecupboard version with instant mash.

INGREDIENTS

Serves 4

300g/11oz/1¼ cups cooked mashed potatoes
200g/7oz can tuna fish in soya oil, drained
115g/4oz/¾ cup canned or frozen sweetcorn
30ml/2 tbsp chopped fresh parsley
50g/2oz/1 cup fresh white or brown breadcrumbs
salt and black pepper
lemon wedges, to serve

1 Place the mashed potato in a bowl and stir in the tuna fish, sweetcorn and chopped parsley.

2 Season to taste with salt and pepper, then shape into eight patty shapes with your hands.

3 Spread out the breadcrumbs on a plate and press the fish cakes into the breadcrumbs to coat lightly, then place on a baking sheet.

4 Cook the fish cakes under a moderately hot grill until crisp and golden brown, turning once. Serve hot with lemon wedges and fresh vegetables.

COOK'S TIP
For simple storecupboard variations which are just as nutritious, try using canned sardines, red or pink salmon, or smoked mackerel in place of the tuna.

NUTRITION NOTES	
Per portion:	
Energy	203Kcals/852kJ
Fat	4.62g
Saturated fat	0.81g
Cholesterol	21.25mg
Fibre	1.82g

THAI-STYLE CHICKEN SALAD

This salad comes from Chiang Mai, a city in the north-east of Thailand. It's hot and spicy, and wonderfully aromatic. Choose strong-flavoured leaves, such as curly endive or rocket, for the salad.

INGREDIENTS

Serves 6

450g/1lb minced chicken breast
1 lemon grass stalk, finely chopped
3 kaffir lime leaves, finely chopped
4 red chillies, seeded and chopped
60ml/4 tbsp lime juice
30ml/2 tbsp fish sauce
15ml/1 tbsp roasted ground rice
2 spring onions, chopped
30ml/2 tbsp coriander leaves
mixed salad leaves, cucumber and
    tomato slices, to serve
mint sprigs, to garnish

1 Heat a large non-stick frying pan. Add the minced chicken and cook in a little water.

2 Stir constantly until cooked, which will take about 7–10 minutes.

3 Transfer the cooked chicken to a large bowl and add the rest of the ingredients. Mix thoroughly.

4 Serve on a bed of mixed salad leaves, cucumber and tomato slices, garnished with mint sprigs.

COOK'S TIP

Use sticky (glutinous) rice to make roasted ground rice. Put the rice in a frying pan and dry roast until golden brown. Remove and grind to a powder with a pestle and mortar or in a food processor. Keep in a glass jar in a cool dry place and use as required.

NUTRITION NOTES

Per portion:

Energy	106Kcals/446kJ
Fat	1.13g
Saturated Fat	0.28g
Cholesterol	52.5mg
Fibre	0.7g

HADDOCK AND BROCCOLI CHOWDER

A warming main-meal soup for hearty appetites.

INGREDIENTS

Serves 4

4 spring onions, sliced
450g/1 lb new potatoes, diced
300ml/½ pint/1¼ cups fish stock or
    water
300ml/½ pint/1¼ cups skimmed milk
1 bay leaf
225g/8oz/2 cups broccoli florets, sliced
450g/1 lb smoked haddock fillets,
    skinned
198g/7oz can sweetcorn, drained
black pepper
chopped spring onions, to garnish

1 Place the spring onions and potatoes in a large saucepan and add the stock, milk and bay leaf. Bring the soup to the boil, then cover the pan and simmer for 10 minutes.

2 Add the broccoli to the pan. Cut the fish into bite-sized chunks and add to the pan with the sweetcorn.

3 Season the soup well with black pepper, then cover the pan and simmer for a further 5 minutes, or until the fish is cooked through. Remove the bay leaf and scatter over the spring onion. Serve hot, with crusty bread.

COOK'S TIP
When new potatoes are not available, old ones can be used, but choose a waxy variety which will not disintegrate.

NUTRITION NOTES

Per portion:

Energy	268Kcals/1124kJ
Fat	2.19g
Saturated fat	0.27g
Cholesterol	57.75mg
Fibre	3.36g

AUBERGINE SALAD

An appetizing and unusual salad that you will find yourself making over and over again.

INGREDIENTS

Serves 6

2 aubergines
15ml/1 tbsp oil
30ml/2 tbsp dried shrimps, soaked
  and drained
15ml/1 tbsp coarsely chopped garlic
30ml/2 tbsp freshly squeezed lime juice
5ml/1 tsp palm sugar
30ml/2 tbsp fish sauce
1 hard-boiled egg, chopped
4 shallots, thinly sliced into rings
coriander leaves, to garnish
2 red chillies, seeded and sliced,
  to garnish

COOK'S TIP
For an interesting variation, try using salted duck's or quail's eggs, cut in half, instead of chopped hen's eggs.

1 Grill or roast the aubergines until charred and tender.

2 When cool enough to handle, peel away the skin and slice the aubergine into thick pieces.

3 Heat the oil in a small frying pan, add the drained shrimps and the garlic and fry until golden. Remove from the pan and set aside.

4 To make the dressing, put the lime juice, palm sugar and fish sauce in a small bowl and whisk together.

5 To serve, arrange the aubergine on a serving dish. Top with the chopped egg, shallot rings and dried shrimp mixture. Drizzle over the dressing and garnish with coriander and red chillies.

NUTRITION NOTES

Per portion:	
Energy	70.5Kcals/295kJ
Fat	3.76g
Saturated Fat	0.68g
Cholesterol	57mg
Fibre	1.20g

MOROCCAN FISH TAGINE

Tagine is actually the name of
the large Moroccan cooking pot
used for this type of cooking, but
you can use an ordinary
casserole instead.

INGREDIENTS

Serves 4
2 garlic cloves, crushed
30ml/2 tbsp ground cumin
30ml/2 tbsp paprika
1 small red chilli (optional)
30ml/2 tbsp tomato purée
60ml/4 tbsp lemon juice
4 cutlets of whiting or cod, about
   175g/6oz each
350g/12oz tomatoes, sliced
2 green peppers, seeded and
   thinly sliced
salt and black pepper
chopped fresh coriander, to garnish

1 Mix together the garlic, cumin,
paprika, chilli, tomato purée and
lemon juice. Spread this mixture over
the fish, then cover and chill for about
30 minutes to let the flavour penetrate.

2 Preheat the oven to 200°C/400°F/
Gas 6. Arrange half of the tomatoes
and peppers in a baking dish.

3 Cover with the fish, in one layer,
then arrange the remaining tomatoes and pepper on top. Cover the
baking dish with foil and bake for
about 45 minutes, until the fish is tender. Sprinkle with chopped coriander
or parsley to serve.

COOK'S TIP
If you are preparing this dish for a
dinner party, it can be assembled
completely and stored in the fridge,
ready to bake when needed.

NUTRITION NOTES

Per portion:	
Energy	203Kcals/855kJ
Fat	3.34g
Saturated fat	0.29g
Cholesterol	80.5mg
Fibre	2.48g

MARINATED CUCUMBER SALAD

Sprinkling cucumbers with salt draws out some of the water and makes them softer and sweeter.

INGREDIENTS

Serves 6

2 medium cucumbers
15ml/1 tbsp salt
90g/3½oz/½ cup granulated sugar
175ml/6fl oz/¾ cup dry cider
15ml/1 tbsp cider vinegar
45ml/3 tbsp chopped fresh dill
pinch of pepper

NUTRITION NOTES

Per portion:

Energy	111Kcals/465kJ
Fat	0.14g
Saturated Fat	0.01g
Fibre	0.62g

1 Slice the cucumbers thinly and place them in a colander, sprinkling salt between each layer. Put the colander over a bowl and leave to drain for 1 hour.

2 Thoroughly rinse the cucumber under cold running water to remove excess salt, then pat dry on absorbent kitchen paper.

COOK'S TIP
As a shortcut, leave out the method for salting cucumber described in step 1.

3 Gently heat the sugar, cider and vinegar in a saucepan, until the sugar has dissolved. Remove from the heat and leave to cool. Put the cucumber slices in a bowl, pour over the cider mixture and leave to marinate for about 2 hours.

4 Drain the cucumber and sprinkle with the dill and pepper to taste. Mix well and transfer to a serving dish. Chill in the fridge until ready to serve.

STUFFED PLAICE ROLLS

Plaice fillets are a good choice for families because they are economical, easy to cook and free of bones. If you prefer, the skin can be removed first.

INGREDIENTS

Serves 4

1 medium courgette, grated
2 medium carrots, grated
60ml/4 tbsp fresh wholemeal
 breadcrumbs
15ml/1 tbsp lime or lemon juice
4 plaice fillets
salt and black pepper

1 Preheat the oven to 200°C/400°F/ Gas 6. Mix together the carrots and courgettes. Stir in the breadcrumbs, lime juice and seasoning.

2 Lay the fish fillets skin side up and divide the stuffing between them, spreading it evenly.

3 Roll up to enclose the stuffing and place in an ovenproof dish. Cover and bake for about 30 minutes, or until the fish flakes easily. Serve hot with new potatoes.

> **COOK'S TIP**
> This recipe creates its own delicious juices, but for an extra sauce, stir chopped fresh parsley into a little low fat fromage frais and serve with the fish.

NUTRITION NOTES

Per portion:

Energy	158Kcals/665kJ
Fat	3.22g
Saturated fat	0.56g
Cholesterol	50.4mg
Fibre	1.94g

WATERCRESS POTATO SALAD BOWL

New potatoes are equally good hot or cold, and this colourful, nutritious salad is an ideal way of making the most of them.

INGREDIENTS

Serves 4

450g/1 lb small new potatoes, unpeeled
1 bunch watercress
200g/7oz/1½ cups cherry tomatoes,
  halved
30ml/2 tbsp pumpkin seeds
45ml/3 tbsp low fat fromage frais
15ml/1 tbsp cider vinegar
5ml/1 tsp soft light brown sugar
salt and paprika

1 Cook the potatoes in lightly salted, boiling water until just tender, then drain and leave to cool.

2 Toss together the potatoes, watercress, tomatoes and pumpkin seeds.

3 Place the fromage frais, vinegar, sugar, salt and paprika in a screw-topped jar and shake well to mix. Pour over the salad just before serving.

NUTRITION NOTES

Per portion:

Energy	150Kcals/630kJ
Fat	4.15g
Saturated fat	0.81g
Cholesterol	0.11mg
Fibre	2.55g

COOK'S TIP
If you are packing this salad for a picnic, take the dressing in the jar and toss in just before serving.

CAJUN-STYLE COD

This recipe works equally well with any firm-fleshed fish – choose low fat fish, such as haddock or monkfish.

NUTRITION NOTES

Per portion:

Energy	137Kcals/577kJ
Protein	28.42g
Fat	1.75g
Saturated Fat	0.26g
Fibre	0.06g

INGREDIENTS

Serves 4

4 cod steaks, each weighing about
*   175g/6oz*
30ml/2 tbsp low fat natural yogurt
15ml/1 tbsp lime or lemon juice
1 garlic clove, crushed
5ml/1 tsp ground cumin
5ml/1 tsp paprika
5ml/1 tsp mustard powder
2.5ml/¹/₂ tsp cayenne pepper
2.5ml/¹/₂ tsp dried thyme
2.5ml/¹/₂ tsp dried oregano
non-stick cooking spray
lemon slices, to garnish
new potatoes and a mixed salad,
*   to serve*

1 Pat the fish dry on kitchen paper. Mix together the yogurt and lime or lemon juice and brush lightly over both sides of the fish.

2 Mix together the crushed garlic, spices and herbs. Coat both sides of the fish with the seasoning mix, rubbing in well.

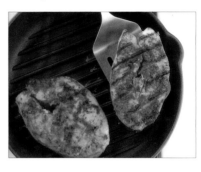

3 Spray a ridged grill pan or heavy-based frying pan with non-stick cooking spray. Heat until very hot. Add the fish and cook over a high heat for 4 minutes, or until the undersides are well browned.

4 Turn the steaks over and cook for a further 4 minutes, or until cooked through. Serve immediately, garnished with lemon and accompanied by new potatoes and a mixed salad.

ROASTED MEDITERRANEAN VEGETABLES

For a really colourful dish, try these vegetables roasted in olive oil with garlic and rosemary. The flavour is wonderfully intense.

INGREDIENTS

Serves 6
1 each red and yellow pepper
2 Spanish onions
2 large courgettes
1 large aubergine or 4 baby aubergines, trimmed
1 fennel bulb, thickly sliced
2 beef tomatoes
8 fat garlic cloves
30ml/2 tbsp olive oil
fresh rosemary sprigs
black pepper
lemon wedges and black olives (optional), to garnish

1 Halve and seed the peppers, then cut them into large chunks. Peel the onions and cut into thick wedges.

NUTRITION NOTES

Per portion:
Energy	120Kcals/504kJ
Fat	5.2g
Saturated Fat	0.68g
Cholesterol	0

2 Cut the courgettes and aubergines into large chunks.

3 Preheat the oven to 220°C/425°F/ Gas 7. Spread the peppers, onions, courgettes, aubergines and fennel in a lightly oiled, shallow ovenproof dish or roasting pan, or, if liked, arrange in rows to make a colourful design.

4 Cut each tomato in half and place, cut-side up, with the vegetables.

5 Tuck the garlic cloves among the vegetables, then brush them with the olive oil. Place some sprigs of rosemary among the vegetables and grind over some black pepper, particularly on the tomatoes.

6 Roast for 20–25 minutes, turning the vegetables halfway through the cooking time. Serve from the dish or on a flat platter, garnished with lemon wedges. Scatter some black olives over the top, if you like.

PLAICE PROVENÇAL

Serves 4
4 large plaice fillets
2 small red onions
120ml/4fl oz/½ cup vegetable stock
60ml/4 tbsp dry red wine
1 garlic clove, crushed
2 courgettes, sliced
1 yellow pepper, seeded and sliced
400g/14oz can chopped tomatoes
15ml/1 tbsp chopped fresh thyme
salt and black pepper
potato gratin, to serve

1 Preheat the oven to 180°C/350°F/
Gas 4. Lay the plaice skin-side
down and, holding the tail end, push a
sharp knife between the skin and flesh
in a sawing movement. Hold the knife
at a slight angle with the blade towards
the skin.

2 Cut each onion into eight wedges.
Put into a heavy-based saucepan
with the stock. Cover and simmer for
5 minutes. Uncover and continue to
cook, stirring occasionally, until the
stock has reduced entirely. Add the
wine and garlic clove to the pan and
continue to cook until the onions
are soft.

3 Add the courgettes, yellow pepper,
tomatoes and thyme and season to
taste. Simmer for 3 minutes. Spoon the
sauce into a large casserole.

COOK'S TIP
Skinless white fish fillets such as
plaice are low in fat and make
an ideal tasty and nutritious basis
for many low fat recipes such as
this one.

4 Fold each fillet in half and put on
top of the sauce. Cover and cook in
the oven for 15–20 minutes, until the
fish is opaque and flakes easily. Serve
with a potato gratin.

NUTRITION NOTES	
Per portion:	
Energy	191Kcals/802kJ
Protein	29.46g
Fat	3.77g
Saturated Fat	0.61g
Fibre	1.97g

SUMMER VEGETABLE BRAISE

Tender, young vegetables are ideal for quick cooking in a minimum of liquid. Use any mixture of the family's favourite vegetables, as long as they are of similar size.

Serves 4

175g/6oz/2½ cups baby carrots
175g/6oz/2 cups sugar-snap peas or
    mangetout
115g/4oz/1¼ cups baby corn cobs
90ml/6 tbsp vegetable stock
10ml/2 tsp lime juice
salt and black pepper
chopped fresh parsley and
    snipped fresh chives, to garnish

1 Place the carrots, peas and baby corn cobs in a large heavy-based saucepan with the vegetable stock and lime juice. Bring to the boil.

2 Cover the pan and reduce the heat, then simmer for 6–8 minutes, shaking the pan occasionally, until the vegetables are just tender.

3 Season the vegetables to taste with salt and pepper, then stir in the chopped fresh parsley and snipped chives. Cook the vegetables for a few seconds more, stirring them once or twice until the herbs are well mixed, then serve at once with grilled lamb chops or roast chicken.

COOK'S TIP
You can make this dish in the winter too, but cut larger, tougher vegetables into chunks and cook for slightly longer.

NUTRITION NOTES

Per portion:	
Energy	36Kcals/152kJ
Fat	0.45g
Saturated fat	0
Cholesterol	0
Fibre	2.35g

MONKFISH AND MUSSEL SKEWERS

Skinless white fish such as monkfish is a good source of protein whilst also being low in calories and fat. These attractive seafood kebabs, flavoured with a light marinade, are excellent grilled or barbecued and served with herby boiled rice and a mixed leaf salad.

INGREDIENTS

Serves 4

450g/1lb monkfish, skinned and boned
5ml/1 tsp olive oil
30ml/2 tbsp lemon juice
5ml/1 tsp paprika
1 garlic clove, crushed
4 turkey rashers
8 cooked mussels
8 raw prawns
15ml/1 tbsp chopped fresh dill
salt and black pepper
lemon wedges, to garnish
salad leaves and long grain and wild rice, to serve

1 Cut the monkfish into 2.5cm/1in cubes and place in a shallow glass dish. Mix together the oil, lemon juice, paprika and garlic clove and season.

2 Pour the marinade over the fish and toss to coat evenly. Cover and leave in a cool place for 30 minutes.

3 Cut the turkey rashers in half and wrap each strip around a mussel. Thread on to skewers, alternating with the fish cubes and raw prawns. Preheat the grill to high.

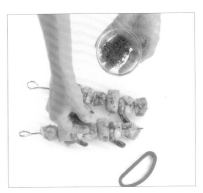

4 Grill the kebabs for 7–8 minutes, turning once and basting with the marinade. Sprinkle with chopped dill and salt. Garnish with lemon wedges and serve with salad and rice.

NUTRITION NOTES	
Per portion:	
Energy	133Kcals/560kJ
Protein	25.46g
Fat	3.23g
Saturated Fat	0.77g
Fibre	0.12g

MIDDLE-EASTERN VEGETABLE STEW

A spiced dish of mixed vegetables which can be served as a side dish or as a vegetarian main course. Children may prefer less chilli.

INGREDIENTS

Serves 4–6
45ml/3 tbsp vegetable or chicken stock
1 green pepper, seeded and sliced
2 medium courgettes, sliced
2 medium carrots, sliced
2 celery sticks, sliced
2 medium potatoes, diced
400g/14oz can chopped tomatoes
5ml/1 tsp chilli powder
30ml/2 tbsp chopped fresh mint
15ml/1 tbsp ground cumin
400g/14oz can chick-peas, drained
salt and black pepper
mint sprigs, to garnish

1 Heat the vegetable or chicken stock in a large flameproof casserole until boiling, then add the sliced pepper, courgettes, carrot and celery. Stir over a high heat for 2–3 minutes, until the vegetables are just beginning to soften.

2 Add the potatoes, tomatoes, chilli powder, mint and cumin. Add the chick-peas and bring to the boil.

3 Reduce the heat, cover the casserole and simmer for 30 minutes, or until all the vegetables are tender. Season to taste with salt and pepper and serve hot garnished with mint leaves.

COOK'S TIP
Chick-peas are traditional in this type of Middle-Eastern dish, but if you prefer, red kidney beans or haricot beans can be used instead.

NUTRITION NOTES

Per portion:
Energy	168Kcals/703kJ
Fat	3.16g
Saturated fat	0.12g
Cholesterol	0
Fibre	6.13g

LEMON SOLE BAKED IN A PAPER CASE

INGREDIENTS

Serves 4

4 lemon sole fillets, each weighing
  about 150g/5oz
½ small cucumber, sliced
4 lemon slices
60ml/4 tbsp dry white wine
sprigs of fresh dill, to garnish
potatoes and braised celery, to serve

For the yogurt hollandaise
150ml/¼ pint low fat natural yogurt
5ml/1 tsp lemon juice
2 egg yolks
5ml/1 tsp Dijon mustard
salt and black pepper

1 Preheat the oven to 180°C/350°F/
Gas 4. Cut out four heart shapes
from non-stick baking paper, each
about 20 x 15cm/8 x 6in.

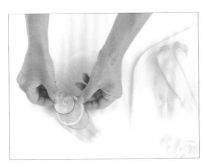

2 Place a sole fillet on one side of
each paper heart. Arrange the
cucumber and lemon slices on top of
each fillet. Sprinkle with the wine and
close the parcels by turning the edges of
the paper and twisting to secure. Put
on a baking tray and cook in the oven
for 15 minutes.

3 Meanwhile make the hollandaise.
Beat together the yogurt, lemon
juice and egg yolks in a double boiler
or bowl placed over a saucepan. Cook
over simmering water, stirring for
about 15 minutes, or until thickened.
(The sauce will become thinner after
10 minutes, but will thicken again.)

COOK'S TIP
Make sure that the paper parcels
are well sealed, so that none of
the delicious juices can escape.

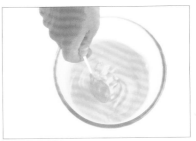

4 Remove from the heat and stir in
the mustard. Season to taste with
salt and pepper. Open the fish parcels,
garnish with a sprig of dill and serve
accompanied with the sauce, new
potatoes and braised celery.

NUTRITION NOTES	
Per portion:	
Energy	185Kcals/779kJ
Protein	29.27g
Fat	4.99g
Saturated Fat	1.58g
Fibre	0.27g

BROCCOLI CAULIFLOWER GRATIN

Broccoli and cauliflower make an attractive combination, and this dish is much lighter than a classic cauliflower cheese.

INGREDIENTS

Serves 4

1 small cauliflower (about 250g/9oz)
1 small head broccoli (about 250g/9oz)
150g/5oz/½ cup natural low fat yogurt
75g/3oz/1 cup grated reduced fat Cheddar cheese
5ml/1 tsp wholegrain mustard
30ml/2 tbsp wholemeal breadcrumbs
salt and black pepper

1 Break the cauliflower and broccoli into florets and cook in lightly salted, boiling water for 8–10 minutes, until just tender. Drain well and transfer to a flameproof dish.

2 Mix together the yogurt, grated cheese and mustard, then season the mixture with pepper and spoon over the cauliflower and broccoli.

3 Sprinkle the breadcrumbs over the top and place under a moderately hot grill until golden brown. Serve hot.

COOK'S TIP
When preparing the cauliflower and broccoli, discard the tougher part of the stalk, then break the florets into even-sized pieces, so they cook evenly.

NUTRITION NOTES

Per portion:

Energy	144Kcals/601kJ
Fat	6.5g
Saturated fat	3.25g
Cholesterol	16.5mg
Fibre	3.25g

STEAMED FISH WITH CHILLI SAUCE

Steaming is one of the best – and lowest fat – methods of cooking fish. By leaving the fish whole and on the bone, you'll find that all the delicious flavour and moistness is retained.

INGREDIENTS

Serves 6

1 large or 2 medium, firm fish like bass or grouper, scaled and cleaned
a fresh banana leaf or large piece of foil
30ml/2 tbsp rice wine
3 red chillies, seeded and finely sliced
2 garlic cloves, finely chopped
2cm/¾in piece of fresh root ginger, finely shredded
2 lemon grass stalks, crushed and finely chopped
2 spring onions, chopped
30ml/2 tbsp fish sauce
juice of 1 lime

For the chilli sauce

10 red chillies, seeded and chopped
4 garlic cloves, chopped
60ml/4 tbsp fish sauce
15ml/1 tbsp sugar
75ml/5 tbsp lime juice

1 Rinse the fish under cold running water. Pat dry with kitchen paper. With a sharp knife, slash the skin of the fish a few times on both sides.

2 Place the fish on the banana leaf or foil. Mix together the remaining ingredients and spread over the fish.

3 Place a small upturned plate in the bottom of a wok or large frying pan, and add about 5cm/2in boiling water. Lay the banana leaf or foil with the fish on top on the plate and cover with a lid. Steam for about 10–15 minutes or until the fish is cooked.

4 Meanwhile, put all the chilli sauce ingredients in a food processor and process until smooth. You may need to add a little cold water.

5 Serve the fish hot, on the banana leaf if liked, with the sweet chilli sauce to spoon over the top.

NUTRITION NOTES	
Per portion:	
Energy	170Kcals/721kJ
Fat	3.46g
Saturated Fat	0.54g
Cholesterol	106mg
Fibre	0.35g

VEGETABLES À LA GRECQUE

This simple side salad is made with winter vegetables, but you can vary it according to the season. This combination of vegetables makes an ideal, low fat side salad to serve with grilled lean meat or poultry, or with thick slices of fresh, crusty bread.

INGREDIENTS

Serves 4

175ml/6fl oz/¾ cup white wine
5ml/1 tsp olive oil
30ml/2 tbsp lemon juice
2 bay leaves
sprig of fresh thyme
4 juniper berries
450g/1lb leeks, trimmed and cut into
*   2.5cm/1in lengths*
1 small cauliflower, broken into florets
4 celery sticks, sliced on the diagonal
30ml/2 tbsp chopped fresh parsley
salt and black pepper

1 Put the wine, oil, lemon juice, bay leaves, thyme and juniper berries into a large, heavy-based saucepan and bring to the boil. Cover and let simmer for 20 minutes.

NUTRITION NOTES	
Per portion:	
Energy	88Kcals/368kJ
Protein	4.53g
Fat	2.05g
Saturated Fat	0.11g
Fibre	4.42g

2 Add the leeks, cauliflower and celery. Simmer very gently for 5–6 minutes or until just tender.

3 Remove the vegetables with a slotted spoon and transfer them to a serving dish. Briskly boil the cooking liquid for 15–20 minutes, or until reduced by half. Strain.

4 Stir the parsley into the liquid and season with salt and pepper to taste. Pour over the vegetables and leave to cool. Chill in the fridge for at least 1 hour before serving.

> COOK'S TIP
> Choose a dry or medium-dry white wine for best results.

BAKED COD WITH TOMATOES

For the very best flavour, use firm sun-ripened tomatoes for the sauce and make sure it is fairly thick before spooning it over the cod.

INGREDIENTS

Serves 4
10ml/2 tsp olive oil
1 onion, chopped
2 garlic cloves, finely chopped
450g/1lb tomatoes, peeled, seeded and chopped
5ml/1 tsp tomato purée
60ml/4 tbsp dry white wine
60ml/4 tbsp chopped flat leaf parsley
4 cod cutlets
30ml/2 tbsp dried breadcrumbs
salt and black pepper
new potatoes and green salad, to serve

NUTRITION NOTES

Per portion:
Energy	151Kcals/647kJ
Fat	1.5g
Saturated Fat	0.2g
Cholesterol	55.2mg
Fibre	2.42g

COOK'S TIP

For extra speed, use a 400g/14oz can of chopped tomatoes in place of the fresh tomatoes and 5–10ml/1–2 tsp ready-minced garlic in place of the garlic cloves.

1 Preheat the oven to 190°C/375°F/ Gas 5. Heat the oil in a pan and fry the onion for about 5 minutes. Add the garlic, tomatoes, tomato purée, wine and seasoning.

2 Bring the sauce just to the boil, then reduce the heat slightly and cook, uncovered, for 15–20 minutes until thick. Stir in the parsley.

3 Grease an ovenproof dish, put in the cod cutlets and spoon an equal quantity of the tomato sauce on to each. Sprinkle the dried breadcrumbs over the top.

4 Bake for 20–30 minutes, basting the fish occasionally with the sauce, until the fish is tender and cooked through, and the breadcrumbs are golden and crisp. Serve hot with new potatoes and a green salad.

KOHLRABI STUFFED WITH PEPPERS

If you haven't sampled kohlrabi, or have only eaten it in stews where its flavour is lost, this dish is recommended. The slightly sharp flavour of the peppers are an excellent foil to the more earthy flavour of the kohlrabi.

INGREDIENTS

Serves 4

4 small kohlrabies, about 175g–225g/
  6–8oz each
about 400ml/14fl oz/1⅔ cup hot
  vegetable stock
15ml/1 tbsp sunflower oil
1 onion, chopped
1 small red pepper, seeded and sliced
1 small green pepper, seeded and sliced
salt and black pepper
flat leaf parsley, to garnish (optional)

NUTRITION NOTES

Per portion:
Energy	112Kcals/470kJ
Fat	4.63g
Saturated Fat	0.55g
Cholesterol	0
Fibre	5.8g

1 Preheat the oven to 180°C/350°F/ Gas 4. Trim and top and tail the kohlrabies and arrange in the base of a medium-sized ovenproof dish.

2 Pour over the stock to come about halfway up the vegetables. Cover and braise in the oven for about 30 minutes, until tender. Transfer to a plate and allow to cool, reserving the stock.

3 Heat the oil in a frying pan and fry the onion for 3–4 minutes over a gentle heat, stirring occasionally. Add the peppers and cook for a further 2–3 minutes, until the onion is lightly browned.

4 Add the reserved vegetable stock and a little seasoning and simmer, uncovered, over a moderate heat until the stock has almost evaporated.

5 Scoop out the insides of the kohl-rabies and chop roughly. Stir into the onion and pepper mixture, taste and adjust the seasoning. Arrange the shells in a shallow ovenproof dish.

6 Spoon the filling into the kohlrabi shells. Put in the oven for 5–10 minutes to heat through and then serve, garnished with a sprig of flat leaf parsley, if liked.

MEDITERRANEAN FISH CUTLETS

These low fat fish cutlets are well complemented by boiled potatoes, broccoli and carrots.

INGREDIENTS

Serves 4

4 white fish cutlets, about 150g/5oz each

about 150ml/¼ pint/⅔ cup fish stock or dry white wine (or a mixture of the two), for poaching

1 bay leaf, a few black peppercorns and a strip of pared lemon rind, for flavouring

For the tomato sauce

400g/14oz can chopped tomatoes

1 garlic clove, crushed

15ml/1 tbsp pastis or other aniseed-flavoured liqueur

15ml/1 tbsp drained capers

12–16 stoned black olives

salt and black pepper

1 To make the sauce, place the chopped tomatoes, garlic, pastis or liqueur, capers and olives in a saucepan. Season to taste with salt and pepper and cook over a low heat for about 15 minutes, stirring occasionally.

2 Place the fish in a frying pan, pour over the stock and/or wine and add the bay leaf, peppercorns and lemon rind. Cover and simmer for 10 minutes or until it flakes easily.

3 Using a slotted spoon, transfer the fish into a heated dish. Strain the stock into the tomato sauce and boil to reduce slightly. Season the sauce, pour it over the fish and serve immediately, sprinkled with the chopped parsley.

COOK'S TIP
Remove skin from cutlets and reduce the quantity of olives to reduce calories and fat. Use 450g/1lb fresh tomatoes, skinned and chopped, in place of the canned tomatoes.

NUTRITION NOTES

Per portion:	
Energy	165Kcals/685kJ
Fat	3.55g
Saturated Fat	0.5g
Cholesterol	69mg

POTATO GRATIN

The flavour of Parmesan is wonderfully strong, so a little goes a long way. Leave the cheese out altogether for an almost fat-free dish.

INGREDIENTS

Serves 4

1 garlic clove
5 large baking potatoes, peeled
45ml/3tbsp freshly grated Parmesan
  cheese
600ml/1 pint/2½ cups vegetable or
  chicken stock
pinch of grated nutmeg
salt and black pepper

1 Preheat the oven to 200°C/400°F/ Gas 6. Halve the garlic clove and rub over the base and sides of a large shallow gratin dish.

2 Slice the potatoes very thinly and arrange a third of them in the dish. Sprinkle with a little grated Parmesan cheese, and season with salt and pepper. Pour over some of the stock to prevent the potatoes from discolouring.

3 Continue layering the potatoes and cheese as before, then pour over the rest of the stock. Sprinkle with the grated nutmeg.

> COOK'S TIP
> For a potato and onion gratin, thinly slice one medium onion and layer with the potato.

4 Bake in the preheated oven for about 1¼–1½ hours or until the potatoes are tender and the tops well browned.

NUTRITION NOTES

Per portion:

Energy	178Kcals/749kJ
Protein	9.42g
Fat	1.57g
Saturated Fat	0.30g
Fibre	1.82g

BAKED FISH IN BANANA LEAVES

Fish that is prepared in this way is particularly succulent and flavourful. Fillets are used here, rather than whole fish, which is easier for those who don't like to mess about with bones. It is a great dish for a barbecue.

INGREDIENTS

Serves 4

250ml/8fl oz/1 cup coconut milk
30ml/2 tbsp red curry paste
45ml/3 tbsp fish sauce
30ml/2 tbsp caster sugar
5 kaffir lime leaves, torn
4 x 175g/6oz fish fillets, such
    as snapper
175g/6oz mixed vegetables, such as
    carrots or leeks, finely shredded
4 banana leaves or pieces of foil
30ml/2 tbsp shredded spring onions, to
    garnish
2 red chillies, finely sliced, to garnish

NUTRITION NOTES

Per portion:
Energy   258Kcals/1094kJ
Fat   4.31g
Saturated Fat   0.7g
Cholesterol   64.75mg
Fibre   1.23g

COOK'S TIP
Coconut milk is low in calories and fat and so makes an ideal basis for a low fat marinade or sauce. Choose colourful mixed vegetables such as carrots, leeks and red pepper, to make the dish more attractive and appealing.

1 Combine the coconut milk, curry paste, fish sauce, sugar and kaffir lime leaves in a shallow dish.

2 Marinate the fish in this mixture for about 15–30 minutes. Preheat the oven to 200°C/400°F/Gas 6.

4 Wrap the fish up by turning in the sides and ends of the leaf and secure with cocktail sticks. (With foil, just crumple the edges together.) Repeat with the rest of the fish.

5 Bake for 20–25 minutes or until the fish is cooked. Alternatively, cook under the grill or on a barbecue. Just before serving, garnish the fish with a sprinkling of spring onions and sliced red chillies.

3 Mix the vegetables together and lay a portion on top of a banana leaf or piece of foil. Place a piece of fish on top with a little of its marinade.

HERBY BAKED TOMATOES

Serves 4–6

675g/1½ lb large red and yellow
   tomatoes
10ml/2 tsp red wine vinegar
2.5ml/½ tsp wholegrain mustard
1 garlic clove, crushed
10ml/2 tsp chopped fresh parsley
10ml/2 tsp snipped fresh chives
25g/1oz/½ cup fresh fine white
   breadcrumbs, for topping
salt and black pepper

NUTRITION NOTES

Per portion:

Energy	37Kcals/156kJ
Fat	0.49g
Saturated Fat	0.16g
Cholesterol	0
Fibre	1.36g

COOK'S TIP
Use wholemeal breadcrumbs in
place of white, for added colour,
flavour and fibre. Use 5–10ml/
1–2 tsp mixed dried herbs, if fresh
herbs are not available.

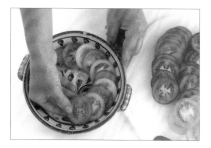

1 Preheat the oven to 200°C/400°F/
Gas 6. Thickly slice the tomatoes
and arrange half of them in a 900ml/
1½ pint/3¾ cup ovenproof dish.

2 Mix the vinegar, mustard, garlic
and seasoning together. Stir in
10ml/2 tsp cold water. Sprinkle the
tomatoes with half the parsley and
chives, then drizzle over half the
dressing.

3 Lay the remaining tomato slices on
top, overlapping them slightly.
Drizzle with the remaining dressing.

4 Sprinkle over the breadcrumbs.
Bake for 25 minutes or until the
topping is golden. Sprinkle with the
remaining parsley and chives. Serve
immediately, garnished with sprigs
of parsley.

MACKEREL KEBABS WITH PARSLEY DRESSING

Oily fish such as mackerel are ideal for grilling as they cook quickly and need no extra oil.

INGREDIENTS

Serves 4

450g/1 lb mackerel fillets
finely grated rind and juice of 1 lemon
45ml/3 tbsp chopped fresh parsley
12 cherry tomatoes
8 pitted black olives
salt and black pepper

1 Cut the fish into 4cm/1½in chunks and place in a bowl with half the lemon rind and juice, half of the parsley and some seasoning. Cover the bowl and leave to marinate for 30 minutes.

2 Thread the chunks of fish on to eight long wooden or metal skewers, alternating them with the cherry tomatoes and olives. Cook the kebabs under a hot grill for 3–4 minutes, turning the kebabs occasionally, until the fish is cooked.

3 Mix the remaining lemon rind and juice with the remaining parsley in a small bowl, then season to taste with salt and pepper. Spoon the dressing over the kebabs and serve hot with plain boiled rice or noodles and a leafy green salad.

> **COOK'S TIP**
> When using wooden or bamboo kebab skewers, soak them first in a bowl of cold water for a few minutes to help prevent them burning.

NUTRITION NOTES

Per portion:

Energy	268Kcals/1126kJ
Fat	19.27g
Saturated fat	4.5g
Cholesterol	61.88mg
Fibre	1g

LEMONY VEGETABLE PARCELS

Serves 4

2 medium carrots
1 small swede
1 large parsnip
1 leek, sliced
finely grated rind of ½ lemon
15ml/1 tbsp lemon juice
15ml/1 tbsp wholegrain mustard
5ml/1 tsp walnut or sunflower oil
salt and black pepper

1 Preheat the oven to 190°C/375°F/ Gas 5. Peel the root vegetables and cut into 1cm/½ in cubes. Place in a large bowl, then add the sliced leek.

2 Stir the lemon rind and juice and the mustard into the vegetables and mix well, then season to taste.

3 Cut four 30cm/12 in squares of non-stick baking paper and brush lightly with the oil.

4 Divide the vegetables among them. Roll up the paper from one side, then twist the ends firmly to seal.

5 Place the parcels on a baking sheet and bake for 50–55 minutes, or until the vegetables are just tender. Serve hot with roast or grilled meats.

NUTRITION NOTES	
Per portion	
Energy	78Kcals/326kJ
Fat	2.06g
Saturated fat	0.08g
Cholesterol	0
Fibre	5.15g

PASTA, PULSES
AND GRAINS

CHINESE SPROUTS

If you are bored with plain boiled Brussels sprouts, try pepping them up with this unusual stir-fried method, which uses the minimum of oil.

INGREDIENTS

Serves 4
450g/1 lb Brussels sprouts, shredded
5ml/1 tsp sesame or sunflower oil
2 spring onions, sliced
2.5ml/½ tsp Chinese five-spice powder
15ml/1 tbsp light soy sauce

1 Trim the Brussels sprouts, then shred them finely using a large sharp knife or shred in a food processor.

2 Heat the oil and add the sprouts and onions, then stir-fry for about 2 minutes, without browning.

3 Stir in the five-spice powder and soy sauce, then cook, stirring, for a further 2–3 minutes, until just tender.

4 Serve hot, with grilled meats or fish, or Chinese dishes.

> COOK'S TIP
> Brussels sprouts are rich in Vitamin C, and this is a good way to cook them to preserve the vitamins. Larger sprouts cook particularly well by this method, and cabbage can also be cooked this way.

NUTRITION NOTES

Per portion:
Energy	58Kcals/243kJ
Fat	2.38g
Saturated fat	0.26g
Cholesterol	0
Fibre	4.67g

LEMON AND HERB RISOTTO CAKE

This unusual rice dish can be served as a main course with salad, or as a satisfying side dish. It's also good served cold, and packs well for picnics.

INGREDIENTS

Serves 4

1 small leek, thinly sliced
600ml/1 pint/2½ cups chicken stock
225g/8oz/1 cup short grain rice
finely grated rind of 1 lemon
30ml/2 tbsp chopped fresh chives
30ml/2 tbsp chopped fresh parsley
75g/3oz/¾ cup grated mozzarella cheese
salt and black pepper
parsley and lemon wedges, to garnish

1 Preheat the oven to 200°C/400°F/ Gas 6. Lightly oil a 22cm/8½ in round, loose-bottomed cake tin.

2 Cook the leek in a large pan with 45ml/3 tbsp stock, stirring over a moderate heat, to soften. Add the rice and the remaining stock.

3 Bring to the boil. Cover the pan and simmer gently, stirring occasionally, for about 20 minutes, or until all the liquid is absorbed.

4 Stir in the lemon rind, herbs, cheese and seasoning. Spoon into the tin, cover with foil and bake for 30–35 minutes or until lightly browned. Turn out and serve in slices, garnished with parsley and lemon wedges.

> COOK'S TIP
> The best type of rice to choose for this recipe is the Italian round grain Arborio rice, but if it is not available, use pudding rice instead.

NUTRITION NOTES

Per portion:
Energy	280Kcals/1176kJ
Fat	6.19g
Saturated fat	2.54g
Cholesterol	12.19mg
Fibre	0.9g

VEGETABLES
AND SALADS

RICE WITH SEEDS AND SPICES

A change from plain boiled rice, and a colourful accompaniment to serve with spicy curries or grilled meats. Basmati rice gives the best texture and flavour, but you can use ordinary long grain rice instead, if you prefer.

INGREDIENTS

Serves 4

5ml/1 tsp sunflower oil
2.5ml/½ tsp ground turmeric
6 cardamom pods, lightly crushed
5ml/1 tsp coriander seeds, lightly crushed
1 garlic clove, crushed
200g/7oz/1 cup basmati rice
400ml/14 fl oz/1⅔ cups stock
115g/4oz/½ cup natural yogurt
15ml/1 tbsp toasted sunflower seeds
15ml/1 tbsp toasted sesame seeds
salt and black pepper
coriander leaves, to garnish

1 Heat the oil in a non-stick pan and fry the spices and garlic for about 1 minute, stirring all the time.

2 Add the rice and stock, bring to the boil then cover and simmer for 15 minutes or until just tender.

3 Stir in the yogurt and the toasted sunflower and sesame seeds. Adjust the seasoning and serve hot, garnished with coriander leaves.

NUTRITION NOTES

Per portion:
Energy	243Kcals/1022kJ
Fat	5.5g
Saturated fat	0.73g
Cholesterol	1.15mg
Fibre	0.57g

COOK'S TIP
Seeds are particularly rich in minerals, so they are a good addition to all kinds of dishes. Light roasting will improve their flavour.

FRUITY HAM AND FRENCH BREAD PIZZA

French bread makes a great pizza base. For a really speedy recipe, use ready-prepared pizza topping instead of the tomato sauce and cook the pizzas under a hot grill for a few minutes to melt the cheese, instead of baking them in the oven.

INGREDIENTS

Serves 4

2 small baguettes
300ml/½ pint/1¼ cups tomato sauce
75g/3oz lean sliced cooked ham
4 canned pineapple rings, drained and chopped
½ small green pepper, seeded and cut into thin strips
50g/2oz reduced fat mature Cheddar cheese
salt and black pepper

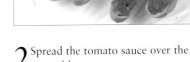

1 Preheat the oven to 200°C/400°F/ Gas 6. Cut the baguettes in half lengthways and toast the cut sides until crisp and golden.

> **COOK'S TIP**
> If you prefer, omit the ham and substitute cooked chicken, peeled prawns or tuna fish.

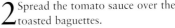

2 Spread the tomato sauce over the toasted baguettes.

3 Cut the ham into strips and lay on the baguettes with the pineapple and green pepper. Season to taste with salt and pepper.

4 Grate the cheese and sprinkle on top. Bake for 15–20 minutes until crisp and golden.

NUTRITION NOTES	
Per portion:	
Energy	111Kcals/468.7kJ
Fat	3.31g
Saturated Fat	1.63g
Cholesterol	18.25mg
Fibre	0.79g

Bulgur and Lentil Pilaf

Bulgur wheat is very easy to cook and can be used in almost any way you would normally use rice, hot or cold. Some of the finer grades need hardly any cooking, so check the pack for cooking times.

INGREDIENTS

Serves 4

5ml/1 tsp olive oil
1 large onion, thinly sliced
2 garlic cloves, crushed
5ml/1 tsp ground coriander
5ml/1 tsp ground cumin
5ml/1 tsp ground turmeric
2.5ml/½ tsp ground allspice
225g/8oz/1¼ cups bulgur wheat
about 750ml/1¼ pints/3⅛ cups stock or water
115g/4oz button mushrooms, sliced
115g/4oz/⅔ cup green lentils
salt, black pepper and cayenne

1 Heat the oil in a non-stick saucepan and fry the onion, garlic and spices for 1 minute, stirring.

2 Stir in the bulgur wheat and cook, stirring, for about 2 minutes, until lightly browned. Add the stock or water, mushrooms and lentils.

3 Simmer over a very low heat for about 25–30 minutes, until the bulgur wheat and lentils are tender and all the liquid is absorbed. Add more stock or water, if necessary.

4 Season well with salt, pepper and cayenne and serve hot.

COOK'S TIP
Green lentils can be cooked without presoaking, as they cook quite quickly and keep their shape. However, if you have the time, soaking them first will shorten the cooking time slightly.

NUTRITION NOTES

Per portion:
Energy	325Kcals/1367kJ
Fat	2.8g
Saturated fat	0.33g
Cholesterol	0
Fibre	3.61g

PAPPARDELLE AND PROVENÇAL SAUCE

INGREDIENTS

Serves 4

2 small red onions
150ml/¼ pint/⅔ cup vegetable stock
1–2 garlic cloves, crushed
60ml/4 tbsp red wine
2 courgettes, cut in fingers
1 yellow pepper, seeded and sliced
400g/14oz can tomatoes
10ml/2 tsp fresh thyme
5ml/1 tsp caster sugar
350g/12oz pappardelle or other
  ribbon pasta
salt and black pepper
fresh thyme and 6 black olives, stoned
  and roughly chopped, to garnish

NUTRITION NOTES

Per portion:

Energy	369Kcals/1550kJ
Fat	2.5g
Saturated Fat	0.4g
Cholesterol	0
Fibre	4.3g

1 Cut each onion into eight wedges through the root end, to hold them together during cooking. Put into a saucepan with the stock and garlic. Bring to the boil, cover and simmer for 5 minutes until tender.

2 Add the red wine, courgettes, yellow pepper, tomatoes, thyme, sugar and seasoning. Bring to the boil and cook gently for 5–7 minutes, shaking the pan occasionally to coat the vegetables with the sauce. (Do not overcook the vegetables as they are much nicer if they remain slightly crunchy.)

3 Cook the pasta in a large pan of boiling, salted water according to the packet instructions, until *al dente*. Drain thoroughly.

4 Transfer the pasta to warmed serving plates and top with the vegetables. Garnish with fresh thyme and chopped black olives.

BASIC PASTA DOUGH
To make fresh pasta, sift 200g/7oz/1¼ cups plain flour and a pinch of salt on to a work surface and make a well in the centre. Break two eggs into the well, together with 10ml/2 tsp of cold water. Using a fork, beat the eggs gently, then gradually draw in the flour from the sides to make a thick paste. When the mixture becomes too stiff to use a fork, use your hands to mix to a firm dough. Knead for 5 minutes until smooth. Wrap in clear film and leave to rest for 20–30 minutes before rolling out and cutting.

MINTED COUSCOUS CASTLES

Couscous is a fine semolina made from wheat grain, which is usually steamed and served plain with a rich meat or vegetable stew. Here it is flavoured with mint and moulded to make an unusual accompaniment to serve with any savoury dish.

INGREDIENTS

Serves 6

225g/8oz/1¼ cups couscous
475ml/16 fl oz/2 cups boiling stock
15ml/1 tbsp lemon juice
2 tomatoes, diced
30ml/2 tbsp chopped fresh mint
oil, for brushing
salt and black pepper
mint sprigs, to garnish

1 Place the couscous in a bowl and pour over the boiling stock. Cover the bowl and leave to stand for 30 minutes, until all the stock is absorbed and the grains are tender.

2 Stir in the lemon juice with the tomatoes and chopped mint. Adjust the seasoning with salt and pepper.

3 Brush the insides of four cups or individual moulds with oil. Spoon in the couscous mixture and pack down firmly. Chill for several hours.

4 Turn out and serve cold, or alternatively, cover and heat gently in a low oven or microwave, then turn out and serve hot, garnished with mint.

COOK'S TIP
Most packet couscous is now the ready cooked variety, which can be cooked as above, but some types need steaming first, so check the pack instructions.

NUTRITION NOTES

Per portion:

Energy	95Kcals/397kJ
Fat	0.53g
Saturated fat	0.07g
Cholesterol	0
Fibre	0.29g

PASTA WITH CHICK-PEA SAUCE

This is a delicious, and very speedy, low fat dish. The quality of canned pulses and tomatoes is so good that it is possible to transform them into a very fresh tasting pasta sauce in minutes. Choose whatever pasta shapes you like, although hollow shapes, such as penne (quills) or shells are particularly good with this sauce.

INGREDIENTS

Serves 6

450g/1lb penne or other pasta shapes
30ml/2 tsp olive oil
1 onion, thinly sliced
1 red pepper, seeded and sliced
400g/14oz can chopped tomatoes
425g/15oz can chick-peas
30ml/2 tbsp dry vermouth (optional)
5ml/1 tsp dried oregano
1 large bay leaf
30ml/2 tbsp capers
salt and black pepper
fresh oregano, to garnish

COOK'S TIP
Choose fresh or dried unfilled pasta for this dish. Whichever you choose, cook it in a large saucepan of water, so that the pasta keeps separate and doesn't stick together. Fresh pasta takes about 2–4 minutes to cook and dried pasta about 8–10 minutes. Cook pasta until it is *al dente* – firm and neither too hard nor too soft.

NUTRITION NOTES

Per portion:

Energy	268Kcals/1125kJ
Fat	2.0g
Saturated Fat	0.5g
Cholesterol	1.3mg
Fibre	4.3g

1 Boil the pasta as instructed on the packet, then drain. Meanwhile, heat the oil in a large saucepan and gently fry the onion and pepper for about 5 minutes, stirring occasionally, until softened.

2 Add the tomatoes, chick-peas with their liquid, vermouth (if liked), herbs and capers and stir well.

3 Season to taste and bring to the boil, then simmer for about 10 minutes. Remove the bay leaf and mix in the pasta. Reheat and serve hot, garnished with sprigs of oregano.

CRACKED WHEAT AND MINT SALAD

Serves 4

250g/9oz/1⅔ cups cracked wheat
4 tomatoes
4 small courgettes, thinly sliced
  lengthways
4 spring onions, sliced on the diagonal
8 ready-to-eat dried apricots, chopped
40g/1½oz/¼ cup raisins
juice of 1 lemon
30ml/2 tbsp tomato juice
45ml/3 tbsp chopped fresh mint
1 garlic clove, crushed
salt and black pepper
sprig of fresh mint, to garnish

1 Put the cracked wheat into a large bowl. Add enough boiling water to come 2.5cm/1in above the level of the wheat. Leave to soak for 30 minutes, then drain well and squeeze out any excess water in a clean dish towel.

2 Meanwhile, plunge the tomatoes into boiling water for 1 minute and then into cold water. Slip off the skins. Halve, remove the seeds and cores and roughly chop the flesh.

3 Stir the chopped tomatoes, courgettes, spring onions, apricots and raisins into the cracked wheat.

4 Put the lemon and tomato juice, mint, garlic clove and seasoning into a small bowl and whisk together with a fork. Pour over the salad and mix well. Chill for at least 1 hour. Serve garnished with a sprig of mint.

NUTRITION NOTES	
Per portion:	
Energy	293Kcals/1231.7kJ
Fat	1.69g
Saturated Fat	0.28g
Fibre	2.25g

SWEET AND SOUR PEPPERS WITH PASTA

A tasty and colourful low
fat dish – perfect for lunch
or supper.

INGREDIENTS

Serves 4

1 red, 1 yellow and 1 orange pepper
1 garlic clove, crushed
30ml/2 tbsp capers
30ml/2 tbsp raisins
5ml/1 tsp wholegrain mustard
rind and juice of 1 lime
5ml/1 tsp clear honey
30ml/2 tbsp chopped fresh coriander
225g/8oz pasta bows
salt and black pepper
shavings of Parmesan cheese, to serve
(optional)

1 Quarter the peppers and remove the stalks and seeds. Put the quarters into boiling water and cook for 10–15 minutes, until tender. Drain and rinse under cold water, then peel off the skin and cut the flesh into strips lengthways.

2 Put the garlic, capers, raisins, mustard, lime rind and juice, honey, coriander and seasoning into a bowl and whisk together.

3 Cook the pasta in a large pan of boiling, salted water for 10–12 minutes, until *al dente*. Drain thoroughly.

4 Return the pasta to the pan and add the pepper strips and dressing. Heat gently, tossing to mix. Transfer to a warm serving bowl and serve with a few shavings of Parmesan cheese, if using.

NUTRITION NOTES	
Per portion:	
Energy	268Kcals/1125kJ
Fat	2.0g
Saturated Fat	0.5g
Cholesterol	1.3mg
Fibre	4.3g

CHILLI BEAN BAKE

The contrasting textures of sauce, beans, vegetables and a crunchy cornbread topping make this a memorable meal.

INGREDIENTS

Serves 4

225g/8oz/1¼ cups red kidney beans
1 bay leaf
1 large onion, finely chopped
1 garlic clove, crushed
2 celery sticks, sliced
5ml/1 tsp ground cumin
5ml/1 tsp chilli powder
400g/14oz can chopped tomatoes
15ml/1 tbsp tomato purée
5ml/1 tsp dried mixed herbs
15ml/1 tbsp lemon juice
1 yellow pepper, seeded and diced
salt and black pepper
mixed salad, to serve

For the cornbread topping
175g/6oz/1½ cups corn meal
15ml/1 tbsp wholemeal flour
5ml/1 tsp baking powder
1 egg, beaten
175ml/6fl oz/¾ cup skimmed milk

1 Soak the beans overnight in cold water. Drain and rinse well. Pour 1 litre/1¾ pints/4 cups water into a large, heavy-based saucepan, add the beans and bay leaf and boil rapidly for 10 minutes. Lower the heat, cover and simmer for 35–40 minutes or until the beans are tender.

NUTRITION NOTES

Per portion:

Energy	399Kcals/1675kJ
Protein	22.86g
Fat	4.65g
Saturated Fat	0.86g
Fibre	11.59g

2 Add the onion, garlic, celery, cumin, chilli powder, chopped tomatoes, tomato purée and dried mixed herbs. Half cover the pan with a lid and simmer for a further 10 minutes.

3 Stir in the lemon juice, yellow pepper and seasoning. Simmer for a further 8–10 minutes, stirring occasionally, until the vegetables are just tender. Discard the bay leaf and spoon the mixture into a large casserole.

4 Preheat the oven to 220°C/425°F/ Gas 7. To make the topping, put the corn meal, flour, baking powder and a pinch of salt into a bowl and mix together. Make a well in the centre and add the egg and milk. Mix and pour over the bean mixture. Bake in the oven for 20 minutes or until brown. Serve hot with mixed salad.

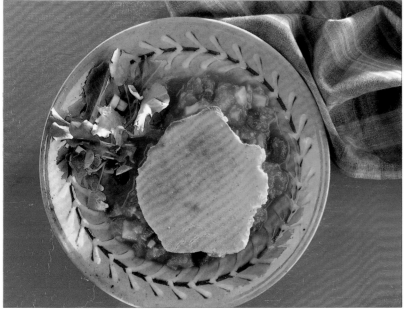

RATATOUILLE PENNE BAKE

Serves 6
1 small aubergine
2 courgettes, thickly sliced
200g/7oz firm tofu, cubed
45ml/3 tbsp dark soy sauce
1 garlic clove, crushed
10ml/2 tsp sesame seeds
1 small red pepper, seeded and sliced
1 onion, finely chopped
1–2 garlic cloves, crushed
150ml/¼ pint/⅔ cup vegetable stock
3 firm ripe tomatoes, skinned, seeded
    and quartered
15ml/1 tbsp chopped mixed herbs
225g/8oz penne or other pasta shapes
salt and black pepper
crusty bread, to serve

1 Wash the aubergine and cut into 2.5cm/1in cubes. Put into a colander with the courgettes, sprinkle with salt and leave to drain for 30 minutes.

3 Put the pepper, onion and garlic into a saucepan with the stock. Bring to the boil, cover and cook for 5 minutes until tender. Remove the lid and boil until all the stock has evaporated. Add the tomatoes and herbs to the pan and cook for a further 3 minutes, then add the rinsed aubergine and courgettes and cook until tender. Season to taste.

4 Meanwhile, cook the pasta in a large pan of boiling, salted water according to the packet instructions, until *al dente*, then drain thoroughly. Preheat the grill. Toss the pasta with the vegetables and tofu. Transfer to a shallow ovenproof dish and grill until lightly toasted. Serve with bread.

2 Mix the tofu with the soy sauce, garlic and sesame seeds. Cover and marinate for 30 minutes.

COOK'S TIP
Tofu is a low fat protein, but it is very bland. Marinating adds plenty of flavour – make sure you leave it for the full 30 minutes.

NUTRITION NOTES	
Per portion:	
Energy	208Kcals/873kJ
Fat	3.7g
Saturated Fat	0.5g
Cholesterol	0
Fibre	3.9g

SPICY BEAN HOT POT

Serves 4

225g/8oz/3 cups button mushrooms
15ml/1 tbsp sunflower oil
2 onions, sliced
1 garlic clove, crushed
15ml/1 tbsp red wine vinegar
400g/14oz can chopped tomatoes
15ml/1 tbsp tomato purée
15ml/1 tbsp Worcestershire sauce
15ml/1 tbsp wholegrain mustard
15ml/1 tbsp soft dark brown sugar
250ml/8fl oz/1 cup vegetable stock
400g/14oz can red kidney
   beans, drained
400g/14oz can haricot or cannellini
   beans, drained
1 bay leaf
75g/3oz/½ cup raisins
salt and black pepper
chopped fresh parsley, to garnish

1 Wipe the mushrooms, then cut them into small pieces. Set aside.

2 Heat the oil in a large saucepan or flameproof casserole, add the onions and garlic and cook over a gentle heat for 10 minutes until soft.

3 Add all the remaining ingredients except the mushrooms and seasoning. Bring to the boil, lower the heat and simmer for 10 minutes.

4 Add the mushrooms and simmer for 5 minutes more. Stir in salt and pepper to taste. Transfer to warm plates and sprinkle with parsley.

NUTRITION NOTES	
Per portion:	
Energy	280Kcals/1175kJ
Fat	4.5g
Saturated Fat	0.5g
Cholesterol	0

SPAGHETTI BOLOGNESE

Serves 8

1 onion, chopped

2–3 garlic cloves, crushed

300ml/½ pint/1¼ cups beef or
  chicken stock

450g/1lb extra-lean minced turkey
  or beef

2 x 400g/14oz cans chopped tomatoes

5ml/1 tsp dried basil

5ml/1 tsp dried oregano

60ml/4 tbsp tomato purée

450g/1lb button mushrooms, quartered
  and sliced

150ml/¼ pint/⅔ cup red wine

450g/1lb spaghetti

salt and black pepper

NUTRITION NOTES

Per portion:

Energy	321Kcals/1350kJ
Fat	4.1g
Saturated Fat	1.3g
Cholesterol	33mg
Fibre	2.7g

1 Put the chopped onion and garlic into a non-stick saucepan with half of the stock. Bring to the boil and cook for 5 minutes until the onion is tender and the stock has reduced completely.

COOK'S TIP
Sautéing vegetables in fat-free stock rather than oil is an easy way of saving calories and fat. Choose fat-free stock to reduce even more.

2 Add the turkey or beef and cook for 5 minutes, breaking up the meat with a fork. Add the tomatoes, herbs and tomato purée, bring to the boil, then cover and simmer for 1 hour.

3 Meanwhile, cook the mushrooms in a non-stick saucepan with the wine for 5 minutes or until the wine has evaporated. Add the mushrooms to the meat with salt and pepper to taste.

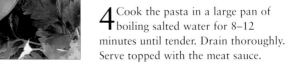

4 Cook the pasta in a large pan of boiling salted water for 8–12 minutes until tender. Drain thoroughly. Serve topped with the meat sauce.

BEAN PURÉE WITH GRILLED CHICORY

The slightly bitter flavours of the radicchio and chicory make a wonderful marriage with the creamy bean purée. Walnut oil adds a nutty taste, but olive oil could also be used.

COOK'S TIP
Other suitable pulses to use are haricot, mung or broad beans.

INGREDIENTS

Serves 4

400g/14oz can cannellini beans
45ml/3 tbsp low fat fromage frais
finely grated rind and juice of
  1 large orange
15ml/1 tbsp finely chopped
  fresh rosemary
4 heads of chicory
2 medium heads of radicchio
10ml/2 tbsp walnut oil
shreds of orange rind, to garnish
  (optional)

1 Drain the beans, rinse, and drain again. Purée the beans in a blender or food processor with the fromage frais, orange rind, orange juice and rosemary. Set aside.

2 Cut the heads of chicory in half lengthwise.

3 Cut each radicchio head into eight wedges. Preheat the grill.

4 Lay out the chicory and radicchio on a baking tray and brush with the walnut oil. Grill for 2–3 minutes. Serve with the purée and scatter over the orange shreds, if using.

NUTRITION NOTES	
Per portion:	
Energy	103Kcals/432kJ
Protein	6.22g
Fat	1.54g
Saturated Fat	0.4g
Fibre	6.73g

PINEAPPLE AND GINGER NOODLE SALAD

The tastes of the tropics are brought together in this appetizing noodle salad, ideal served as a lunch or suppertime dish.

INGREDIENTS

Serves 4

275g/10oz dried udon noodles
½ pineapple, peeled, cored and sliced
  into 4cm/1½in rings
45ml/3 tbsp soft light brown sugar
60ml/4 tbsp fresh lime juice
60ml/4 tbsp coconut milk
30ml/2 tbsp fish sauce
30ml/2 tbsp grated fresh root ginger
2 garlic cloves, finely chopped
1 ripe mango or 2 peaches, finely diced
black pepper
2 spring onions, finely sliced, 2 red
  chillies, seeded and finely shredded,
  plus mint leaves, to garnish

NUTRITION NOTES

Per portion:
Energy	350Kcals/1487kJ
Fat	4.49g
Saturated Fat	0.05g
Cholesterol	0
Fibre	3.13g

COOK'S TIP
Use 4–6 canned pineapple rings in fruit juice, if fresh pineapple is not available. If you haven't any fresh garlic, use 10ml/2 tsp ready-minced garlic instead. Choose ripe mangoes that have a smooth, unblemished skin and give slightly when you squeeze them gently.

1 Cook the noodles in a large saucepan of boiling water until tender, following the directions on the packet. Drain, then refresh under cold water and drain again.

3 Mix the lime juice, coconut milk and fish sauce in a salad bowl. Add the remaining brown sugar, with the ginger and garlic, and whisk well. Add the noodles and pineapple.

2 Place the pineapple rings in a flameproof dish, sprinkle with 30ml/2 tbsp of the sugar and grill for about 5 minutes, or until golden. Cool slightly and cut into small dice.

4 Add the mango or peaches to the bowl and toss well. Scatter over the spring onions, chillies and mint leaves before serving.

LENTIL BOLOGNESE

A really useful sauce to serve with pasta, as a pancake stuffing or even as a protein-packed sauce for vegetables.

INGREDIENTS

Serves 6
45ml/3 tbsp olive oil
1 onion, chopped
2 garlic cloves, crushed
2 carrots, coarsely grated
2 celery sticks, chopped
115g/4oz/²⁄₃ cup red lentils
400g/14oz can chopped tomatoes
30ml/2 tbsp tomato purée
450ml/³⁄₄ pint/2 cups stock
15ml/1 tbsp fresh marjoram, chopped,
  or 5ml/1 tsp dried marjoram
salt and black pepper

1 Heat the oil in a large saucepan and gently fry the onion, garlic, carrots and celery for about 5 minutes, until they are soft.

NUTRITION NOTES

Per portion:

Energy	103Kcals/432kJ
Fat	2.19g
Saturated Fat	0.85g
Fibre	2.15g

2 Add the lentils, tomatoes, tomato purée, stock, marjoram and seasoning to the pan.

3 Bring the mixture to the boil, then partially cover with a lid and simmer for 20 minutes until thick and soft. Use the sauce as required.

COOK'S TIP
You can easily reduce the fat in this recipe by using less olive oil, or substituting a little of the stock and cooking the vegetables over a low heat in a non-stick frying pan until they are soft.

Spaghetti with Chilli Bean Sauce

A nutritious vegetarian option, ideal as a low fat main course.

Nutrition Notes

Per portion:
Energy	431Kcals/1811kJ
Fat	3.6g
Saturated Fat	0.2g
Cholesterol	0
Fibre	9.9g

Ingredients

Serves 6

1 onion, finely chopped
1–2 garlic cloves, crushed
1 large green chilli, seeded
  and chopped
150ml/¼ pint/⅔ cup vegetable stock
400g/14oz can chopped tomatoes
30ml/2 tbsp tomato purée
120ml/4fl oz/½ cup red wine
5ml/1 tsp dried oregano
200g/7oz French beans, sliced
400g/14oz can red kidney
  beans, drained
400g/14oz can cannellini
  beans, drained
400g/14oz can chick-peas, drained
450g/1lb spaghetti
salt and black pepper

1 To make the sauce, put the chopped onion, garlic and chilli into a non-stick pan with the stock. Bring to the boil and cook for 5 minutes until tender.

2 Add the tomatoes, tomato purée, wine, seasoning and oregano. Bring to the boil, cover and simmer the sauce for 20 minutes.

3 Cook the French beans in boiling, salted water for about 5–6 minutes until tender. Drain thoroughly.

4 Add all the beans and the chick-peas to the sauce and simmer for a further 10 minutes. Meanwhile, cook the spaghetti in a large pan of boiling, salted water according to the individual packet instructions, until *al dente*. Drain thoroughly. Transfer the pasta to a serving dish or plates and top with the chilli bean sauce.

> **Cook's Tip**
> Rinse canned beans thoroughly under cold, running water to remove as much salt as possible and drain well before use.

COCONUT RICE

A delicious alternative to plain boiled rice, brown or white rice will both work well.

INGREDIENTS

Serves 6
450g/1lb/2 cups long grain rice
250ml/8fl oz/1 cup water
475ml/16fl oz/2 cups coconut milk
2.5ml/½ tsp salt
30ml/2 tbsp granulated sugar
fresh shredded coconut, to garnish

1 Wash the rice in cold water until it runs clear. Place the water, coconut milk, salt and sugar in a heavy-based saucepan or flameproof casserole.

COOK'S TIP
Coconut milk is available in cans, but if you cannot find it, use creamed coconut mixed with water according to the packet instructions.

2 Add the rice, cover and bring to the boil. Reduce the heat to low and simmer for about 15–20 minutes or until the rice is tender to the bite and cooked through.

3 Turn off the heat and allow the rice to rest in the saucepan for a further 5–10 minutes.

4 Fluff up the rice with chopsticks or a fork before serving garnished with shredded coconut.

NUTRITION NOTES	
Per portion:	
Energy	322.5Kcals/1371kJ
Fat	2.49g
Saturated Fat	1.45g
Cholesterol	0
Fibre	0.68g

PASTA PRIMAVERA

You can use any mixture of fresh, young spring vegetables to make this delicately flavoured pasta dish.

INGREDIENTS

Serves 4

225g/8oz thin asparagus spears, chopped in half
115g/4oz mange-tout, topped and tailed
115g/4oz baby sweetcorn
225g/8oz whole baby carrots, trimmed
1 small red pepper, seeded and chopped
8 spring onions, sliced
225g/8oz torchietti or other pasta shapes
150ml/¼ pint/⅔ cup low fat cottage cheese
150ml/¼ pint/⅔ cup low fat yogurt
15ml/1 tbsp lemon juice
15ml/1 tbsp chopped parsley
15ml/1 tbsp snipped chives
skimmed milk (optional)
salt and black pepper
sun-dried tomato bread, to serve

1 Cook the asparagus spears in a pan of boiling, salted water for 3–4 minutes. Add the mange-tout halfway through the cooking time. Drain and rinse both under cold water to stop further cooking.

2 Cook the baby corn, carrots, red pepper and spring onions in the same way until tender. Drain and rinse.

3 Cook the pasta in a large pan of boiling, salted water according to the packet instruction, until *al dente*. Drain thoroughly.

4 Put the cottage cheese, yogurt, lemon juice, parsley, chives and seasoning into a food processor or blender and process until smooth. Thin the sauce with skimmed milk, if necessary. Put into a large pan with the pasta and vegetables, heat gently and toss carefully. Serve at once with sun-dried tomato bread.

NUTRITION NOTES	
Per portion:	
Energy	320Kcals/1344kJ
Fat	3.1g
Saturated Fat	0.4g
Cholesterol	3mg
Fibre	6.2g

JASMINE RICE

Perfectly cooked rice makes an ideal, low fat accompaniment to many low fat dishes such as vegetable chilli and vegetable bolognese.

INGREDIENTS

Serves 6
450g/1lb/2 cups long grain rice
750ml/1¼ pints/3 cups cold water
2.5ml/½ tsp salt

NUTRITION NOTES

Per portion:
Energy	270.8Kcals/1152kJ
Fat	0.75g
Saturated Fat	0
Cholesterol	0
Fibre	0.37g

COOK'S TIP

An electric rice cooker both cooks the rice and keeps it warm. Different sizes and models are available. The top of the range is a non-stick version, which is expensive, but well worth the money if you eat rice a lot.

2 Put the rice in a heavy-based saucepan or flameproof casserole and add the water and salt. Bring the rice to a vigorous boil, uncovered, over a high heat.

3 Stir and reduce the heat to low. Cover and simmer for up to 20 minutes, or until all the water has been absorbed. Remove from the heat and leave to stand for 10 minutes.

1 Rinse the rice in several changes of cold water until the water stays clear.

4 Remove the lid and stir the rice gently with chopsticks or a fork to fluff up and separate the grains.

TAGLIATELLE WITH MUSHROOMS

Serves 4

1 small onion, finely chopped
2 garlic cloves, crushed
150ml/¼ pint/⅔ cup vegetable stock
225g/8oz mixed fresh mushrooms, such
    as field, chestnut, oyster or
    chanterelles
60ml/4 tbsp white or red wine
10ml/2 tsp tomato purée
15ml/1 tbsp soy sauce
5ml/1 tsp chopped fresh thyme
30ml/2 tbsp chopped fresh parsley, plus
    extra to garnish
225g/8oz fresh sun-dried tomato and
    herb tagliatelle
salt and black pepper
shavings of Parmesan cheese, to serve
    (optional)

1 Put the onion and garlic into a pan with the stock, then cover and cook for 5 minutes or until tender.

NUTRITION NOTES

Per portion:

Energy	241Kcals/1010kJ
Fat	2.4g
Saturated Fat	0.7g
Carbohydrate	45g
Fibre	3g

2 Add the mushrooms (quartered or sliced if large or left whole if small), wine, tomato purée and soy sauce. Cover and cook for 5 minutes.

3 Remove the lid from the pan and boil until the liquid has reduced by half. Stir in the chopped fresh herbs and season to taste.

4 Cook the fresh pasta in a large pan of boiling, salted water for 2–5 minutes until *al dente*. Drain thoroughly and toss lightly with the mushrooms. Serve, garnished with parsley and shavings of Parmesan cheese, if you like.

SPINACH AND HAZELNUT LASAGNE

A vegetarian dish which is hearty enough to satisfy meat-eaters too. Use frozen spinach if you're short of time.

INGREDIENTS

Serves 4

900g/2 lb fresh spinach
300ml/½ pint/1¼ cups vegetable or
  chicken stock
1 medium onion, finely chopped
1 garlic clove, crushed
75g/3oz/¼ cup hazelnuts
30ml/2 tbsp chopped fresh basil
6 sheets lasagne
400g/14oz can chopped tomatoes
200g/7oz/1 cup low fat fromage frais
flaked hazelnuts and chopped parsley,
  to garnish

1 Preheat the oven to 200°C/400°F/ Gas 6. Wash the spinach and place in a pan with just the water that clings to the leaves. Cook the spinach on a fairly high heat for 2 minutes until wilted. Drain well.

2 Heat 30ml/2 tbsp of the stock in a large pan and simmer the onion and garlic until soft. Stir in the spinach, hazelnuts and basil.

3 In a large ovenproof dish, layer the spinach, lasagne and tomatoes. Season well between the layers. Pour over the remaining stock. Spread the fromage frais over the top.

4 Bake the lasagne for about 45 minutes, or until golden brown. Serve hot, sprinkled with lines of flaked hazelnuts and chopped parsley.

> **COOK'S TIP**
> The flavour of hazelnuts is improved by roasting. Place them on a baking sheet and bake in a moderate oven, or under a hot grill, until light golden.

NUTRITION NOTES

Per portion:

Energy	365Kcals/1532kJ
Fat	17g
Saturated fat	1.46g
Cholesterol	0.5mg
Fibre	8.16g

FUSILLI WITH SMOKED TROUT

INGREDIENTS

Serves 4–6

2 carrots, cut in julienne sticks
1 leek, cut in julienne sticks
2 celery sticks, cut in julienne sticks
150ml/¹/₄ pint/²/₃ cup vegetable or
  fish stock
225g/8oz smoked trout fillets, skinned
  and cut into strips
200g/7oz low fat cream cheese
150ml/¹/₄ pint/²/₃ cup medium sweet
  white wine or fish stock
15ml/1 tbsp chopped fresh dill
  or fennel
225g/8oz fusilli (long, corkscrew pasta)
salt and black pepper
dill sprigs, to garnish

1 Put the carrots, leek and celery into a pan with the vegetable or fish stock. Bring to the boil and cook quickly for 4–5 minutes until the vegetables are tender and most of the stock has evaporated. Remove from the heat and add the smoked trout.

NUTRITION NOTES	
Per portion:	
Energy	339Kcals/1422kJ
Fat	4.7g
Saturated Fat	0.8g
Cholesterol	57mg
Fibre	4.1g

2 To make the sauce, put the cream cheese and wine or fish stock into a saucepan, heat and whisk until smooth. Season with salt and pepper. Add the chopped dill or fennel.

3 Cook the pasta according to the packet instructions in a large pan of boiling, salted water until *al dente*. Drain thoroughly.

4 Return the pasta to the pan with the sauce, toss lightly and transfer to a serving bowl. Top with the cooked vegetables and trout. Serve at once garnished with dill sprigs.

COOK'S TIP
When making the sauce, it is important to whisk it continuously while heating, to ensure a smooth result. Smoked salmon may be used in place of the trout, for a tasty change.

CALZONE

INGREDIENTS

Makes 4
450g/1 lb/4 cups plain flour
pinch of salt
1 sachet easy-blend yeast
about 350ml/12 fl oz/1½ cups warm
  water

For the filling
5ml/1 tsp olive oil
1 medium red onion, thinly sliced
3 medium courgettes, about 350g/12oz
  total weight, sliced
2 large tomatoes, diced
150g/5oz mozzarella cheese, diced
15ml/1 tbsp chopped fresh oregano
skimmed milk, to glaze
salt and black pepper

1 To make the dough, sift the flour and salt into a bowl and stir in the yeast. Stir in just enough warm water to mix to a soft dough.

2 Knead for 5 minutes until smooth. Cover and leave in a warm place for about 1 hour, or until doubled in size.

3 Meanwhile, to make the filling, heat the oil and sauté the onion and courgettes for 3–4 minutes. Remove from the heat and add the tomatoes, cheese, oregano and seasoning.

4 Preheat the oven to 220°C/425°F/ Gas 7. Knead the dough lightly and divide into four. Roll out each piece on a lightly floured surface to a 20cm/8in round and place a quarter of the filling on one half.

5 Brush the edges with milk and fold over to enclose the filling. Press firmly to enclose. Brush with milk.

6 Bake on an oiled baking sheet for 15–20 minutes. Serve hot or cold.

NUTRITION NOTES

Per portion:

Energy	544Kcals/2285kJ
Fat	10.93g
Saturated fat	5.49g
Cholesterol	24.42mg
Fibre	5.09g

CRAB PASTA SALAD

Low fat yogurt makes a piquant dressing for this salad.

INGREDIENTS

Serves 6

350g/12oz pasta twists
1 small red pepper, seeded and
    finely chopped
2 x 175g/6oz cans white crab
    meat, drained
115g/4oz cherry tomatoes, halved
1/4 cucumber, halved, seeded and sliced
    into crescents
15ml/1 tbsp lemon juice
300ml/1/2 pint/1 1/4 cups low fat yogurt
2 celery sticks, finely chopped
10ml/2 tsp horseradish cream
2.5ml/1/2 tsp paprika
2.5ml/1/2 tsp Dijon mustard
30ml/2 tbsp sweet tomato pickle
    or chutney
salt and black pepper
fresh basil, to garnish

1 Cook the pasta in a large pan of boiling, salted water, according to the instructions on the packet, until *al dente*. Drain and rinse thoroughly under cold water.

NUTRITION NOTES	
Per portion:	
Energy	305Kcals/1283kJ
Fat	2.5g
Saturated Fat	0.5g
Cholesterol	43mg
Fibre	2.9g

2 Cover the chopped red pepper with boiling water and leave to stand for 1 minute. Drain and rinse under cold water. Pat dry on kitchen paper.

3 Drain the crab meat and pick over carefully for pieces of shell. Put into a bowl with the halved tomatoes and sliced cucumber. Season with salt and pepper and sprinkle with lemon juice.

4 To make the dressing, add the red pepper to the yogurt, with the celery, horseradish cream, paprika, mustard and sweet tomato pickle or chutney. Mix the pasta with the dressing and transfer to a serving dish. Spoon the crab mixture on top and garnish with fresh basil.

TURKEY AND MACARONI CHEESE

A tasty low fat alternative to macaroni cheese, the addition of turkey rashers ensures this dish is a family favourite. Serve with warm ciabatta bread and a mixed leaf salad.

---- NUTRITION NOTES ----

Per portion:

Energy	152Kcals/637kJ
Fat	2.8g
Saturated Fat	0.7g
Cholesterol	12mg
Fibre	1.1g

INGREDIENTS

Serves 4

1 medium onion, chopped
150ml/¼ pint/⅔ cup vegetable or chicken stock
25g/1oz/2 tbsp low fat margarine
45ml/3 tbsp plain flour
300ml/½ pint/¼ cup skimmed milk
50g/2oz reduced fat Cheddar cheese, grated
5ml/1 tsp dry mustard
225g/8oz quick-cook macaroni
4 smoked turkey rashers, cut in half
2–3 firm tomatoes, sliced
a few fresh basil leaves
15ml/1 tbsp grated Parmesan cheese
salt and black pepper

1 Put the chopped onion and stock into a non-stick frying pan. Bring to the boil, stirring occasionally and cook for 5–6 minutes or until the stock has reduced entirely and the onion is transparent.

2 Put the margarine, flour, milk and seasoning into a saucepan and whisk together over the heat until thickened and smooth. Draw aside and add the cheese, mustard and onion.

3 Cook the macaroni in a large pan of boiling, salted water according to the instructions on the packet. Preheat the grill. Drain thoroughly and stir into the sauce. Transfer to a shallow, oven-proof dish.

4 Arrange the turkey rashers and tomatoes overlapping on top of the macaroni cheese. Tuck in the basil leaves, then sprinkle with Parmesan and grill to lightly brown the top.

PASTA WITH TOMATO AND TUNA

Serves 6

1 medium onion, finely chopped
1 celery stick, finely chopped
1 red pepper, seeded and diced
1 garlic clove, crushed
150ml/¼ pint/⅔ cup chicken stock
400g/14oz can chopped tomatoes
15ml/1 tbsp tomato purée
10ml/2 tsp caster sugar
15ml/1 tbsp chopped fresh basil
15ml/1 tbsp chopped fresh parsley
450g/1lb pasta shells
400g/14oz canned tuna in
    brine, drained
30ml/2 tbsp capers in vinegar, drained
salt and black pepper

1 Put the chopped onion, celery, red pepper and garlic into a pan. Add the stock, bring to the boil and cook for 5 minutes or until the stock has reduced almost completely.

2 Add the tomatoes, tomato purée, sugar and herbs. Season to taste and bring to the boil. Simmer for about 30 minutes until thick, stirring occasionally.

3 Meanwhile, cook the pasta in a large pan of boiling, salted water according to the packet instructions, until *al dente*. Drain thoroughly and transfer to a warm serving dish.

COOK'S TIP
If fresh herbs are not available, use a 400g/14oz can of chopped tomatoes with herbs and add 5–10ml/1–2 tsp mixed dried herbs, in place of the fresh herbs.

4 Flake the tuna fish into large chunks and add to the sauce with the capers. Heat gently for 1–2 minutes, pour over the pasta, toss gently and serve immediately.

NUTRITION NOTES

Per portion:

Energy	369Kcals/1549kJ
Fat	2.1g
Saturated Fat	0.4g
Cholesterol	34mg
Fibre	4g